SAINTS&
SINNERS

SAINTS&SINNERS

A Journalist's 50 Years
of Third World Wonders

BY PETER A. GENIESSE

SAINTS & SINNERS
A JOURNALIST'S 50 YEARS OF THIRD WORLD WONDERS

iUniverse books may be ordered through booksellers or by contacting:

iUniverse
1663 Liberty Drive
Bloomington, IN 47403
www.iuniverse.com
1-800-Authors (1-800-288-4677)

ISBN: 978-1-4917-9932-1 (sc)
ISBN: 978-1-4917-9933-8 (e)

Print information available on the last page.

iUniverse rev. date: 07/21/2016

To Antonio, Santiago and Máximo

*May the generation
of my grandsons
promote peace and justice
throughout the world.*

CONTENTS

Preface

I sometimes wonder where I would be today if I had received that commission to fly F-86s for the U.S. Air Force back in the fall of 1960. I had passed a battery of mental and physical tests and I was gung-ho to get to Lackland AFB in Texas for flight training. The Vietnam War was on the horizon, and I was anxious to serve my county.

There was only one thing standing in my way. I was 1-A, right at the top of my draft board's list. I got their notice in the mail before I got to flight school. It trumped my Air Force invitation. So I quickly signed up with the Army Reserves for six months of active duty at Fort Leonard Wood, Missouri, rather than face the unknown in the Army on a two-year draft stint.

I was a college grad and an Army combat engineer grunt and I remember slogging through the infiltration course beneath barbed wire fences and live rounds while glancing at the contrails of fighter jets marking their territory in the blue sky.

I did have some down moments, but I survived the threats of the Berlin Crisis and Cuba's Bay of Pigs. I was on alert but I never left Missouri.

I wonder where I would be today if I had gotten that job at the *New York Times* when I was discharged. I had applied earlier, and was offered a job as a copy boy for $45 a week. However, I was advised to come back after I had fulfilled my military obligations.

But then came a national military freeze. I couldn't leave my Army Reserve unit in Green Bay, Wis. So I reluctantly accepted a job at a Catholic diocesan weekly newspaper, and while waiting for the thaw, I wrote a persuasive piece about the need for Papal Volunteers in Latin America.

In the summer of 1963, as Vietnam was ablaze, I suddenly wasn't so gung-ho to go to war. Rather, an adventure as a lay missionary somewhere in South America somehow seemed more appealing. My Army Reserve unit in Green Bay graciously deferred my military obligation so I could join the Papal Volunteers for a three-year mission tour of duty in northern Chile.

I was a pioneer in the lay apostolate experiment that evolved from the Second Vatican Council. Pope John XXIII called for diocesan and religious orders to dedicate 10 per cent of their numbers to bolstering the faith in Latin America. The goal was to send 20,000 priests, religious and lay people south of the border by the year 1970.

Five years into the program, only 1,622 had signed up. In 1965, there were 400 Papal Volunteers in the field and their numbers were in decline, dropping to just 251 two years later.

The program needed new blood, and a young priest from Sioux City, Iowa, Father Raymond Kevane, was named national director of PAVLA in 1964. He set out to put his conservative stamp on the lay apostolate. He moved his offices to Chicago, drew up a seven-point plan to resurrect the program, got the nod of a committee of bishops and set out to see for himself how the volunteers were faring in missions throughout Latin America.

He was unprepared for the reaction he aroused by his insistence that Papal Volunteers were to be "agents of support" for the local bishops. He said he faced opposition from proponents of liberation theology and *"Comunidades de Base"* who were dedicated to change in the Church.

Everywhere he went he heard missionaries sing the praises of Msgr. Ivan Illich and Father Gustavo Gutierrez, O.P., who were promoting *"desarollo"* (change) and the Church's "preferential option for the poor."

Kevane claimed that Illich's sessions for missionaries in Cuernavaca, Mexico, were devoted to indoctrinating students in communism. So he cut off PAVLA's connection to Illich's schools and established his own training center at Catholic University in Washington, D.C., along with a language school in Mexico City.

The first year the summer program drew 60 volunteers and 70 more were added the second year. The number grew to 300 in the field, and Latin American bishops had submitted requests for 2,000 more volunteers.

But Kevane couldn't convince his hierarchal critics in the U.S. that he was on the right track. "I worked among priests and bishops who were completely enslaved by the heresies of Americanism and Modernism," he said.

"They were out to destroy PAVLA because they feared it would interfere with their intention to implant a Marxist philosophy in the Church and in all countries of Latin America."

He added, "There also were those who did not want to see the power of the lay apostolate unleashed in support of the Church."

Kevane was ordered to move PAVLA's headquarters to Washington, D.C., in the fall of 1967 so his program could be monitored more closely. Then his budget was cut, and his training center faced reviews.

"I began to realize that I was up against a massive organization that promoted liberation theology, which was a thinly veiled form of Marxism," he said.

On July 1, 1969, Kevane met with a committee of bishops and handed in his resignation. One year later, PAVLA, the Catholic Church's lay apostolate experiment, was swiftly terminated.

"The Papal Volunteer program would have ushered into the Church a group of laity who were dedicated to bringing harmony with bishops and priests," Kevane said. "A great opportunity was lost when the bishops failed to act to forestall its destruction."

Kevane returned to the diocesan offices in Sioux City, Iowa, where he served as chancellor for three years. Then he sought laicization and married a woman he knew early in his priestly career. In 2012, he published a 568-page memoir entitled: "Betrayed: An American Priest

Speaks Out," which details his struggles during his five-year stint as PAVLA's National Director.

Meanwhile, in the summer of 1963, I was being radicalized at Ivan Illich's boot camp for missionaries in Cuernavaca, Mexico. My eyes were being opened to the misdeeds of the U.S. throughout Latin America. My rote Catholicism was being challenged on the eve of the Second Vatican Council.

I had 16-plus years of Catholic schooling, including four at Notre Dame, but I wasn't prepped for radical social justice. My father was a conservative Catholic who faithfully read "The Wanderer." I was the youngest of five, with a brother who was a priest and two sisters who were nuns.

Who was I to question the church's teachings? But question I did.

When I arrived in Cuernavaca, I thought Christopher Columbus was a hero and the United States of America could do no wrong. I was soon proven wrong on both counts. We were lectured daily by the who's who of revolutionary thought, and I bought into their message.

When I landed in Antofagasta, Chile, a mining capital and a hotbed of communism, I joined the natives who took to the streets to protest U.S. rule and Anaconda Co.'s control of Chile's vast copper reserves.

Two years later, when I returned to the United States, I joined the protests against the Vietnam War, the same war in which I longed to fly fighter jets five years earlier.

My life had come full circle.

INTRODUCTION

For much of my life, I wanted to be a foreign correspondent. Exotic travels, exciting news, a journalist's dream job.

In my younger days, I followed a newsman's track. I put out a neighborhood paper when I was 10 and then I was on the staff of my high school and college publications. I was a cop reporter for the South Bend Tribune on the graveyard shift, and worked for a Catholic weekly in Green Bay, Wis. Ink was in my blood.

However, fate interfered with my plans. Military orders kept me homebound in the early 1960s. The *New York Times* wouldn't pay me a living wage. A girlfriend — then a wife — detoured me from a correspondent gig in Lima, Peru. And family illness put an end to my wanderlust.

Upon my return from Chile in the fall of 1965, I applied for a reporter's job at the Appleton, WI *Post-Crescent*, and spent the next 30 years in various editor slots from whence I was to embark on my dream.

In the summer of 1986, I caught a break. The Contra War was raging in Nicaragua, and Wisconsin had a stake in President Reagan's venture. Since I was the only staffer who could speak Spanish, I was invited to join a state contingent to make sense of the dichotomy. I wrote an eight-part series, "Inside Nicaragua," for the paper, and I was off and running.

The following year I was in Cuba with a religious group. I signed news credentials for two of the members and invited myself along for the ride. The result was an eight-part series, "Inside Cuba."

Next was a 10-day media tour of Israel, sponsored by a Zionist group, with interviews of leading politicos, including Yitzhak Rabin, featured in "Inside Israel." Then came Haiti and Guyana, Vietnam and India, and repeat tours of Nicaragua, Cuba and Haiti.

I remember meeting Terrence Smith at the Hotel Montana bar in Port au Prince during the boatlifts which drew hordes of newsmen to Haiti. Smith was a classmate of mine at Notre Dame and he had gone on to be a famous journalist with the *New York Times*. "Why in the world would Appleton, Wisconsin, care about Haiti?" he wondered. "It doesn't," I replied. "But I do!"

Ever since my lay missionary days, I've been both intrigued and disturbed about poverty in Third World countries. Why was Haiti the most impoverished nation in the hemisphere when it once was the single richest colony in the world? Haiti won its independence from the French in 1803, but it never had a free election until 1990.

I befriended two young Haitians who were attending Fox Valley Technical College in Appleton, Wis., on a two-year program for poor but promising students from the Caribbean. They invited me to visit their country to tell their stories.

When I retired from The Post-Crescent, I continued to travel and free-lance write about Third World countries. I visited Guyana with a Food for the Poor contingent. I returned to Chile to trace my footprints 40 years later.

I traveled to the Himalayas of India on a Hindu pilgrimage with a famed guru, whose daughter lived in Appleton. I returned to Vietnam with a young refugee girl, a boatperson whom I had sponsored in 1981. Her story, "Cuc: Flower of the Delta," became my first book.

My second book, "Illegal: NAFTA refugees forced to flee," answered the question why millions of undocumented Mexicans had come to the U.S.

Mexico has become our second home. My wife, Jill, and I honeymooned in Acapulco in 1969 and we've returned two dozen times to all parts of the country. Our daughter-in-law, Leticia, is from a remote village in the foothills south of Tampico. She and our son, Peter, and their three boys "vacation" there every year.

Everywhere I traveled in the Third World, my press card introduced me to important and inspiring people.

I was on the platform in downtown Antofagasta, Chile, with presidential candidate Salvador Allende, and I recall shaking hands with Augusto Pinochet long before he was made general.

I had coffee with Yitzhak Rabin in Jerusalem and was in court for the Holocaust trial of "Ivan the Terrible" Demjanjuk. I traveled with the "Witness for Peace" founder Gail Phares and was on the podium with President Daniel Ortega in Managua, Nicaragua.

I was in the crowd to hear Fidel Castro rant for hours in downtown Havana, Cuba, and I called Haiti's President Jean-Bertrand Aristide on his home phone. I was in Santiago, Chile, when St. Alberto Hurtado was canonized and I was baptized in the Ganges in India by Guru Sant Keshavadas.

I was in San Cristobol, Mexico, when "Red" Bishop Samuel Ruiz was under siege, and I was in Madison, Wisconsin, when the 14th Dalai Lama came to call. I met "Liberation Theologian" Gustavo Gutierrez in Cuernavaca, Mexico, and rallied with Oscar Romero followers at the School of the Americas at Fort Benning, Georgia.

As a journalist, I had the best of both worlds. For a couple of weeks each year, I vacationed in the Third World as a foreign correspondent, and met fascinating characters and witnessed global events. The rest of the year, I was home in time for supper.

CHAPTER ONE

Photo by Peter A. Geniesse

A group of nuns in modified holiday garb training for mission work in 1963 takes time to celebrate at a religious festival at Chalma, not far from Msgr. Ivan Illich's missionary outpost in Cuernavaca, Mexico.

"We must acknowledge that missioners can be pawns in a world ideological struggle, and that it is blasphemous to use the gospel to prop up any social or political system."
--Ivan Illich

CHAPTER ONE

'ICONOCLAST' IVAN ILLICH

1926-2002
Cuernavaca, Mexico   1963

"*Yanqui*, go home!"

It was three in the morning, even before the roosters started to crow, and a deranged man pounding on a metal trashcan roamed the halls shouting at the gringos who had just arrived from the U.S. to take part in a four-month missionary boot camp.

We really didn't know what to expect when we signed up to study Spanish and learn all about the culture and mores of Latin Americans. We had heard tales about that mad Russian who ran the school. But who was this guy in the long white gown and pointed hood, and why was he telling us to go home?

His name was Msgr. Ivan Illich, a brilliant, controversial Catholic priest still in his 30s, sent by Francis Cardinal Spellman of New York to prepare the way for the deluge of Puerto Ricans flooding America. He had been named vice rector of Catholic University of Puerto Rico where his outspokenness landed him in trouble. He then fled to a friendlier diocese in Mexico where his assigned task was to prepare priests, nuns and laypeople to serve the Catholic Church throughout Latin America.

We didn't know it at the time, but his self-assignment was to send us back to the U.S., or at least teach us a lesson for life. He feared we would carry our American baggage to a people still struggling to cure

1

the Spanish hangover. Latin America just didn't need a new wave of *conquistadores,* he said. He meant it when he shouted "Yanqui go home!"

Just three years earlier, Pope John XXIII put out a call for North American missionaries to "modernize" the Latin American Church. Religious orders and dioceses were urged to send 10 per cent of their numbers to bolster the faith of the underserved Latinos south of the border.

We were excited to be part of the mission. Illich was noticeably disturbed.

He had established the Center for Intercultural Documentation (CIDOC) in Cuernavaca ostensibly to prepare missionaries for their new roles, teaching them Spanish and bringing them up to date on customs and culture.

There were 30 of us, equal numbers of priests, nuns and laypeople, all living under one roof. The "non-religious" mostly were Papal Volunteers for Latin America, or PAVLA. Lay missionaries were a new experiment for the Church, and it was, indeed, a work in progress.

From the beginning, Illich strived to turn around the papal program. He was open with his intentions. He wanted to challenge the recruits to face reality, refuse their assignments or at least be "a little bit less unprepared." Later he recalled, "We wanted to dissuade the mission-sponsoring agencies from implementing Pope John XXIII's plan."

In 1967, Illich penned a polemic piece entitled "The Seamy Side of Charity" for *America* magazine, the Jesuits' national Catholic review. It was time, he said, to assess the program and its need for sending thousands of missionaries and millions of dollars south of the border.

"Church policy makers in the United States must face up to the socio-political consequences involved in their well-intentioned missionary ventures," he wrote. "They must review their vocation as Christian theologians and their actions as Western politicians. Men and money sent with missionary motivation carry a foreign Christian image, a foreign pastoral approach and a foreign political message," he said.

"It also turns bishops into abject beggars," he added.

"We must acknowledge that missioners can be pawns in a world ideological struggle and that it is blasphemous to use the gospel to prop up any social or political system."

Illich foresaw disaster with another round of foreign invaders. He feared the new wave of gringos would Americanize the church. He became determined to weed out those who weren't willing to be incarnated to the cause. Besides, as a revolutionary, he subscribed to the phoenix theory of change. A new church would rise from the ashes if its future wasn't burdened and way-laid with Band Aid solutions.

So he sent letters to bishops and religious superiors saying their candidates were not qualified, and they should be recalled home.

This did not set well with those leaders. They believed in the people they sent. Their cries didn't take long to reach the Vatican. Illich was called in to face an inquisition, and before the decade was over, his school was closed to future missionaries.

Illich then turned CIDOC into a think tank for socio-economic research and a base for lectures as well as a place to write volumes of scathing social criticism.

Illich was born in 1926 and raised in Vienna until the occupying Nazis expelled his family in 1941. His father was Croatian Catholic but his mother was a Sephardic Jew. By the time he was nine, he was fluent in French, German and Italian. But he was rejected by a top school in Vienna that labeled him as retarded. So he spent his youth in his grandfather's library voraciously reading and teaching himself other languages. By the time he was ready for college, he had mastered a half-dozen other idioms, including Latin and Greek.

He enrolled at the University of Florence, and then decided to enter the priesthood, studying theology and philosophy at the Gregorian University in Rome. He received a doctorate degree from the University of Salzburg, with a historical focus on the institutionalization of the Catholic Church in the 13th century.

He met Thomist philosopher Jacques Maritain, who was French ambassador to the Vatican, at a seminar in Rome. Through him he became acquainted with Giovanni Battista Montini, the future Pope

Paul VI, who urged him to join the Vatican diplomatic corps. Illich declined, preferring to follow Maritain to Princeton University.

He was ordained a priest in 1951 in Rome, celebrated his first Mass in the catacombs, and then he was off to New York. There he met Francis Cardinal Spellman and was assigned to a parish in Washington Heights, which was populated by Irish immigrants and recently arrived Puerto Ricans. He taught himself Spanish and soon he was speaking out for the Puerto Ricans and against "cultural ignorance."

His parish years came to a close in 1956 with the massive fiesta of San Juan, the patron saint of Puerto Rico, which drew more than 35,000 Puerto Ricans to Fordham University.

Cardinal Spellman took a liking to the energetic young priest with a cause, and as thousands of Puerto Ricans continued to pour into New York, he sent Illich to Puerto Rico to prepare the way for priests in the archdiocese to minister to their needs. He also made Illich the youngest monsignor in the U.S. to underscore his credibility.

Illich was named vice rector of the Catholic University in Ponce but he only lasted four years. He publicly clashed with two bishops who had planned to form a political party to oppose Gov. Luis Munoz Marin because he wouldn't forbid the sale of contraceptives on the island. Illich insisted the bishops had no call to meddle in politics.

He was forced out of the university in 1960, and was recalled to New York and Fordham University where he founded the Center for Intercultural Formation to train American missionaries to work in Latin America. He soon moved the Center to Cuernavaca, Mexico, where under the direction of Feodora Stancioff and Bro. Gerry Morris, the school trained several hundred missionaries before being closed down by the Vatican.

The Center evolved into much more than a language and culture school. It became an international magnet for intellectuals and revolutionaries, who would spend a week or more lecturing the students and promoting change at Illich's "thinkery." German psychologist Eric Fromm was a regular. So was Gustavo Gutiérrez, the Peruvian priest who penned Liberation Theology. Father Leo Mahan, a Chicago priest who established an experimental parish in Panama, often gave presentations.

It was a heady lineup of who's who in the mission fields of Latin America. We were constantly challenged, stimulated and often shocked, with revolutionary ideas. Some of the students had no use for the sessions. Others stayed well into the night, drinking Cuba Libres and conversing with those icons they previously had known through their writings.

It was an intensive program. Four hours of Spanish repetition, one tutor to two students, each morning, followed by four hours of Latin American history, culture, economics, politics and religious practices. The lectures sometimes were in Spanish or French or German, with earphone translations by Illich's multi-lingual staff.

On weekends, we were encouraged to take to the road, ride a third class bus anywhere, get to know real people. Sometimes we were lined up to spend Friday and Saturday nights with a Mexican family – from across the spectrum.

One time I was assigned to stay in a desperate slum in Mexico City, tin and cardboard shacks without electricity, no running water, and with shared outdoor privies. I slept on a mat on the dirt floor, fending off a turkey and a pig and three wide-eyed boys with whom I shared a plate of beans and rice.

The following weekend was a different story. The address I was given was in Chapultepec, the richest enclave in Mexico City. The family lived in a mansion, their teenage daughter drove a Mercedes, and that night she was celebrating her *quinceañera* at a posh hotel with 100 of her closest friends. The following day we ended up at their vacation home in Cuernavaca, a bouganvilla-walled estate with a huge swimming pool and a tennis court.

Illich banned the nuns and priests from wearing religious garb at the Center or out in public, a law that lingered from the days when the Mexican government persecuted Catholic clergy in the 1920s. Some sisters who hadn't been out of uniform since they first entered the convent were upset. At first they felt uncomfortable in blouses and skirts that accented their tan marks, but by the end of four months, most welcomed the transition.

Not all the students, priests, nuns and laypeople bought into the CIDOC program. But I did. I was ecstatic. It was the best education I'd received in 16 years of Catholic schooling. Here I was taught to think.

Illich often was at odds with Church leaders. But the Vatican took special notice when he said he was out to "deinstitutionalize the Church in Latin America." Then there was that Benedictine Monastery in Cuernavaca that put its monks through psychoanalysis with most of them purged overnight. The "Red Bishop" of Morelos, Sergio Mendez Arceo, a close friend of Illich, also was in the Vatican's bulls-eye.

On the eve of the Second Vatican Council in 1963, Illich gathered his "thinkery" team and drew up agendas on the future of the Catholic Church. Many of the proposals already had been put into practice at CIDOC, such as the greater role of the laity and the celebration of the Mass in the vernacular.

We gave them an enthusiastic sendoff to Rome with Mass and mariachis and fireworks into the night. Illich was in his glory as he led his multi-language "thinkery" squad of six laymen to the gates of the Vatican. There, for more than a month, they held forth in a coffee shop, which attracted progressive bishops from Latin America and other Third World countries.

Many of the documents which were promulgated at Vatican II had a hearing at that humble coffee shop just a short walk from St. Peter's Basilica.

Illich returned to Cuernavaca buoyed by the bishops' progressive actions. But he soon came back to earth as he faced renewed opposition from the episcopacy to his shunning of missionaries who wouldn't shed their ethnocentric ways.

He was a prophet, a mystic, a man disciplined in prayer as well as service to mankind. When he celebrated Mass every afternoon, an aura surrounded his being, some saying it was like he had seen a beatific vision at the consecration. However, when the Mass was over, he often regressed as a scary terror.

His "thinkery" often sowed the seeds of change for the poor and oppressed throughout Latin America. The Center's intensive four-month language program was designed to jump start Spanish learning.

Illich took note of its success and his team went to work to formulate intense four-month literacy and mathematics programs, among others. He believed the poor, with the right motivation and creative programs, could overcome years of bondage by the oligarchy in just four months. Generational change for the poor just couldn't wait for college.

Two decades later, his "each one, teach one" literacy program was adopted in Nicaragua and in a matter of a couple of years, the country's literacy rate went from 20 per cent to 80 per cent.

Five years after the Vatican closed down CIDOC's role in training missionaries, my wife Jill and I had breakfast with Illich at his "thinkery." At the time, he had nothing to do with the language school or any other programs on site. However, he had stayed true to his celibacy vows, and his daily recitation of the divine office. He had left the priestly ministry, but not the Catholic Church. For awhile he lived like a hermit in a hut on the outskirts of Cuernavaca. But the Center soon became his haven, an international crossroads for intellectuals, guests who would stay a fortnight or more in deep thought with Illich.

In 1970, Illich published "Deschooling Society," a radical approach to education, which soon became a must read for educators and administrators. His fame spread due to his academic presentations and interviews and essays in *The New York Times, America*, and a variety of foreign publications including *Excelsior de Mexico, Le Monde and The Guardian.*

The success of "Deschooling Society" was followed by more than a dozen books and dissertations that focused on the shortcomings of industrialization, medicine and health care, society and even "The Right to Useful Unemployment."

Illich's influence still is felt throughout Latin America, especially in educational fields. He opened a branch of the CIDOC school in Petropolis, Brazil, to serve the Portuguese-speaking mission. Illich became the first student, becoming fluent in the language within three weeks. He also immersed himself in Brazilian life and culture under the tutelage of progressive Archbishop Helder Camera.

But for all his achievements, he remained a target for conservative critics. The archbishop of Puebla called for his removal in 1967. So did Cardinal Alfredo Ottaviani, former head of the Congregation of the Defense of the Faith. When Illich got wind of a statement by Pope Paul VI that he was a "dangerous figure in the Church," he sent a letter to the pope.

"If I have failed in any way against faith or morality, communicate to me how I have so failed, disposed as I am to immediately retract my mistakes," he wrote.

The following June he was summoned to Rome. He was labeled a heretic and was prohibited from speaking on religious matters for five years. In addition, all nuns and priests were forbidden to attend CIDOC.

Illich resigned from his priestly ministry in 1969. His Center for Intercultural Documentation (CIDOC) continued for another decade, and on Jan. 31, 1976, its last class on economics closed 15 controversial years of seminars questioning the legitimacy of modern institutions. More than 13,000 missionaries, teachers, engineers and other professionals, as well as college students, had taken part in the live-in seminars.

CIDOC's files, documentary collection and specialized library on social change, the Catholic Church and Latin American culture were turned over to El Colegio de Mexico.

Illich continued to write social critiques into the 1980s, books about the economics of scarcity and literacy practices. He later divided his time between Mexico, the United States and Germany. He served as visiting professor of philosophy and of science, technology and society at Penn State University. He also taught at the University of Bremen.

In the early 1990s, he was diagnosed as having cancer. He insisted on administering his own medicine against the advice of physicians, who proposed a largely sedative treatment. "That would have rendered my work impossible," Illich said. He was able to finish a history of pain, which was published in French in 2003, a year after his death.

Illich died in Bremen, Germany, Dec. 2, 2002, at the age of 76.

Resources:

William Spielburger, National Catholic Reporter, "Cuernavaca Era Ends," Feb. 27, 1976.

Editors Lee Hoinacki and Carl Mitcham: "The Challenges of Ivan Illich," A collective reflection; State University of New York Press, 2002

Ivan Illich: "The Right to Useful Unemployment," And its professional enemies; Marion Boyers Publishers, London, 1978.

Ivan Illich: "Deschooling Society"; Harper & Row Publishers, New York, 1972.

Ivan Illich: "The Seamy Side of Charity," America, Jan. 21, 1967

Chapter Two

(Authorized for use by image custodian Jim Hesburgh, his brother)
Father Theodore Hesburgh was president of the University of Notre Dame for 35 years and spent the next 25 years in service to popes and presidents.

"When you are working for justice, for human freedom, for human rights, and for human development you are indeed working for the Kingdom of God."
–Theodore Hesburgh

Chapter Two

ND's Ted Hesburgh

1917-2015
Cuernavaca, Mexico   1963

He was counselor to popes and presidents. He was honored by scores of universities. He was universally admired for his efforts to bring peace and justice to this world.

But if you asked him what he was most proud of in his 90-plus years of life, he'd invariably answer: his priesthood. "I am a priest, first and foremost," he said.

He relished the Old Testament's majestic declarative: "Thou art a priest forever according to the order of Melchizedek." Being a priest means being a mediator and Father Theodore Hesburgh, C.S.C., was, indeed, one of Melchizedek's masterful mediators.

"You have to stand between God and man, between sin and goodness, between ignorance and knowledge, between being uncared for and caring," he said. "You stand in a thousand human situations between God and men, trying to bring the message of God to man, and man's petitions to God.

"It means many temporal things such as civil rights, human justice, human and world development, things I've spent my life doing," Hesburgh said. "I think education is a very priestly activity. I think that anything that brings us from ignorance to knowledge would be seen as a priestly activity."

In 1952, at age 35, Hesburgh was named president of the University of Notre Dame. At the time, it was a relatively small Midwestern Catholic college, known more for football than academics. But the young priest immediately moved Notre Dame toward more rigorous academic standards

"I would rather see Notre Dame die, than be educationally mediocre," he said. "We will be the best, or please God, we will cease to exist here."

Hesburgh dreamed of creating a university commensurate with the vision of John Henry Cardinal Newman, the great priest-intellectual of 19th century English Catholicism.

He raised admission standards, restructured the curriculum, increased graduate enrollment and began a concerted drive for the highest intellectual achievement. When he retired 35 years later, Notre Dame had become a major player in higher education. Under his leadership, the annual operating budget went from $9.6 million to $176 million in 1987. The endowment went from $9 million to $350 million. Enrollment doubled to 9,600 students. The faculty grew from 389 to 951.

In 1967, he was instrumental in shifting the university's governance from the Congregation of Holy Cross to a two-tiered, mixed board of lay and religious trustees. Five years later, Hesburgh opened the doors to women in the institution that had been all-male for more than a century.

He had become a national leader in the field of education, serving on numerous commissions and study groups. He was chairman of the International Federation of Catholic universities from 1963 to 1970 and led the movement to redefine the nature and mission of the contemporary Catholic university. He chaired the Board of Overseers at Harvard University. He also headed the Knight Commission on Intercollegiate Athletics, an influential advocate for reforms in college sports from 1990 to 2003.

His stature as elder statesman in American education is reflected in his 150 honorary degrees, believed to be the most awarded to one person.

And then somehow he found time to serve four popes and 16 presidential appointments.

He was appointed the permanent Vatican representative on the International Atomic Energy Agency in Vienna from 1956 to 1970. At the request of Pope Paul VI, he established the Ecumenical Institute at Tantur, Jerusalem, in 1972, which Notre Dame continues to operate.

He represented the Vatican at the United Nations' human rights declaration in Teheran, Iran, in 1968, and became a member of the Holy See's U.N. delegation six years later. In 1983, Pope John Paul II named Hesburgh to the Pontifical Council for Culture, charging him with finding ways for the Gospel to be preached effectively across the world's variegated cultures.

Hesburgh's 16 presidential appointments involved him in virtually all major social issues: civil rights, peaceful uses of atomic energy, campus unrest, treatment of Vietnam draft evaders, immigration reform and Third World development. He joined the board of the Overseas Development Council which helped to avert mass starvation in Cambodia in 1979-80.

"I have always believed that you have to work for justice on earth and not just in eternity," he said. "We create conditions for the Kingdom of God here on earth in preparation for the kingdom in Heaven.

"When you are working for justice, for human freedom, for human rights and for human development, you are indeed working for the Kingdom of God."

He was a charter member of the U.S. Commission on Civil Rights, appointed by President Dwight D. Eisenhower in 1957. He was named chairman in 1969 by President Richard Nixon, who later dismissed him because "he didn't fit in" with Nixon's "Southern Strategy."

Hesburgh created a "civil rights commission in exile" at Notre Dame's Law School, which houses papers collected during his 15 years on the commission.

President Gerald Ford named Hesburgh to the nine-member Presidential Clemency Board to determine the fate of 113,337 Vietnam-era draft-evaders and military deserters. Hesburgh was considered the conscience of the board.

"I was always in favor of unconditional amnesty simply because the war was ill-begotten in the first place," he said. "It may well be that those who resisted were more courageous from a moral point of view than some of those who went."

In 1979, President Jimmy Carter named Hesburgh as chairman of the 16-member Select Commission on Immigration. Their consensus formed the 1986 Immigration Reform Act. The key pillars were employer sanctions, identity cards, amnesty for illegal aliens and a guest worker program.

Hesburgh was, by definition, a frequent flyer. For most of his life, he kept up an exhausting schedule of meetings and conferences throughout the U.S. and abroad. His appointments weren't honorific. They were work assignments that brought notice and honor to Notre Dame.

Hesburgh's fame and Notre Dame sometimes opened doors in the most unlikely places.

In 1973, shortly after the military coup that deposed Salvador Allende, resulting in his death, Hesburgh flew to Santiago, Chile, to meet with Gen. Augusto Pinochet.

Pinochet, head of the military junta, had installed himself as chief of state and was flexing his muscles over the private sector. He threatened to expropriate St. George's College, a major parochial high school in Santiago, owned and administered by the Congregation of the Holy Cross, Notre Dame's Chile connection.

He demanded a private meeting with the ruthless dictator. He told Pinochet that if he went through with his plans, Hesburgh would make sure that the general would be an anathema in Chile and within the Catholic Church worldwide. His position wouldn't be just uncomfortable, Hesburgh said, "but in a word untenable."

Pinochet, who attended Catholic schools as a youth, listened to the priest and backed down on his plans.

Hesburgh often went out of his way to support Notre Dame's alumni in need. José Napoleon Duarte, a member of a leading family in El Salvador, was a theology student and friend of Hesburgh at Notre Dame. He graduated in 1948.

Duarte was first elected president of El Salvador in 1972, winning the election by an overwhelming majority in a country torn by civil war. Shortly after the election, a group of military officers seized power. The police savagely beat Duarte, fracturing his skull and cheekbones. Rolando Duarte, fearing for his brother's life, pleaded with Hesburgh to use his contacts to have José sent to a neutral country.

Hesburgh called a former high ranking officer in California. He told the priest someone would call him within an hour. The caller said Duarte would be sent across the border to Guatemala "in a weakened condition, but he would survive."

The anonymous caller explained, "We got in touch with the presidents of Venezuela and Panama. They called the general in charge of El Salvador and told him that if Duarte did not live, when it was their time to be overthrown and to look for sanctuary, they would see to it that no Latin American country would give them sanctuary."

In May 1985, President Duarte, the first Notre Dame graduate to become head of state, was the commencement speaker and received an honorary degree from his theology professor.

I graduated from the University of Notre Dame in 1960, following in the footsteps of my brother Joe, my father Levi and his brother Oswald, who played football with Knute Rockne's Four Horsemen.

My commencement ceremony featured a U.S. president, a future pope and a living saint: Dwight D. Eisenhower, Giovanni Cardinal Montini (Pope Paul VI) and Tom Dooley, the "Jungle Doctor" of Southeast Asia.

All were acquaintances of Father Hesburgh, who at age 43 already had lots of friends in high places. Hesburgh had been president for just eight years and he was one of the best known clerics in public life.

Still, the student body during my four years at Notre Dame often sent mixed messages about their absentee president, the man with the suitcase on his way to the airport. One lame joke had it that the difference between God and Hesburgh is that Hesburgh is everywhere – except Notre Dame.

But I was a big fan of the man. He was making a name for Notre Dame. He didn't short-change us. He elevated the true nature of Catholic higher education. During my commencement ceremonies, he was on the podium introducing the president, the pope and the saint in front of national media and thousands of parents and guests. I still treasure the moment.

Someday, I said to myself, I'd really like to meet him in person, maybe even have a real conversation.

Three years after graduation from Notre Dame, I was at the Center of Intercultural Documentation in Cuernavaca, Mexico. I was a Papal Volunteer, enlisted in a four-month boot camp with other laymen, priests and religious in training to be missionaries.

One evening the word got out that Father Hesburgh had arrived at the Center. He was only staying a day or so. He was on his way to Chile to check up on a group of Peace Corps volunteers. But first he wanted to meet with Msgr. Ivan Illich to get his take on sending Americans on mission trips.

He had a special fondness for his foster kids. For eight weeks the Peace Corps volunteers had trained on the campus of Notre Dame and Hesburgh had become both friend and advisor to a number of recent college grads who made up one of the first classes of volunteers.

Hesburgh welcomed them to his penthouse suite, high above the 13-story library named in his honor. They often debated sociological and ethical issues well into the night as they sipped rum and Cokes.

It wasn't long after his inaugural that President John Kennedy established the Peace Corps. Hesburgh came on board early in 1961 and offered Notre Dame as the first university to sponsor a training program. There were 42 volunteers, nine from Notre Dame, in that intensive eight-week course that covered language, history, economics and the culture of Chile in the summer of 1961.

Hesburgh had connections in Chile. His Holy Cross religious order operated academic institutions and parishes mostly in the Santiago region. Their members were called upon to assess needs and assignments in the rural areas. Walter Langford, professor of modern languages at Notre Dame, was the field director for the first Peace Corps group to serve Chile until 1963.

Hesburgh praised the program and his charges at a send-off banquet on July 21, 1961. "The Peace Corps offers you a dimension that is lacking in our modern life – a spirit of idealism and adventure," he told his class.

Two years later Hesburgh was on his way to Chile to assess the fruits of their labor. But first he wanted to hear what Illich had to say about the "invasion" of North Americans, whom he labeled the new *conquistadores*.

Illich invited me to sit in on their conversation over breakfast coffee and toasted bolillos. After all, I was a Notre Dame grad and my brother Joe was a Holy Cross priest and a friend of Hesburgh's. Both were interested in what I thought about lay missioners and the Papal Volunteer program.

Illich came down hard on the Catholic Church's missionary plan which called for religious orders to send 10 percent of their members to serve the needs of Latin America. While he could accept lifer missionaries, he feared a surge of unprepared short-term clerics would carry too much baggage and would do more harm than good.

Illich was less critical of lay involvement in the mission. While he couldn't support the United States' Alliance for Progress program of aid for Latin America, labeling it political intrusion, he welcomed the well-prepared, open-minded, enthusiastic youths as described by Hesburgh.

The Peace Corps got his nod; the Papal Volunteers for Latin America, not so much.

I was a member of PAVLA, and I was dismayed by Illich's no-confidence vote. After all, PAVLA was Catholic; the Peace Corps wasn't.

In addition, his Center at the time had PAVLA laymen and several diocesan priests in training to serve missions in Latin America.

Hesburgh wasn't kind toward PAVLA either. He predicted that the lay missioner program was doomed from the start. There was no vision, he said. Nor was there organization, standards, training or money to support and sustain volunteers in the field. He asked me how I was going to get along once I arrived in Northern Chile.

I related that I was to be assigned by the bishop of Antofagasta to teach English in a Catholic elementary school that was vying for students with a nearby Episcopal school. I was likely to live in a rectory. I was financially supported by women auxiliaries from six parishes in the Green Bay Diocese, each one sending me $10 a month. My dad matched that amount.

I had no boss, no supervisor within 1,000 miles. There was only one other PAVLA lay missioner in town, a nurse from Manitowoc, Wis.,who had been transferred after a disastrous assignment in the mountains of Central Mexico.

Hesburgh and Illich both smiled as they listened to my tale, shaking their heads in disbelief. Both predicted an early demise of PAVLA if major steps weren't taken to shore up the program. Maybe you should join the Peace Corps, they said half seriously.

I followed Hesburgh's career through the years with great pride. I visited the Holy Cross Fathers' St. George campus in Santiago, Chile, the staging area for Hesburgh's first Peace Corps volunteers. And back in the United States, I made frequent pilgrimages to the Grotto at Notre Dame where a poignant letter inscribed in bronze from Tom Dooley on his deathbed to Father Hesburgh holds a place of honor.

I fished the musky waters in Land-o-Lakes, Wisconsin, favored by Father Ted, and stayed at the nearby Notre Dame Camp where Hesburgh once sequestered members of the divided U.S. Commission on Civil Rights until they could come to terms with proposed legislation.

I participated in a symposium on Middle East peace talks in the Hesburgh Center's Kroc Institute for International Peace Studies at Notre Dame and followed that up with an hour casual interview with him in his penthouse office atop the Hesburgh Library.

To many, Hesburgh means Notre Dame. He simply made the university what it is today. His first book, entitled "God, Country and Notre Dame," tells of the priorities of the man who prized his vocation as a priest, and a member of the Holy Cross family. His 35 years as university president, the longest tenure in Notre Dame history, was followed by a quarter century of public service which was a credit to his university. He was one of the nation's most influential figures in higher education, the Catholic Church and in national and international affairs.

Hesburgh was in his early 90s when he was forced to slow down. He was a voracious reader but he had lost his sight to macular degeneration. He continued to celebrate daily Mass and was kept up to date by aides in the geriatric wing of Holy Cross House.

He died in his room on the night of Feb. 26, 2015. He was 97 years old.

"We mourn today a great man and faithful priest who transformed the University of Notre Dame," Father John I. Jenkins, C.S.C. said. "With his leadership, charisma and vision, he turned a relatively small Catholic college known for football into one of the nation's great institutions for higher learning."

Notre Dame's president continued, "In his historic service to the nation, the Church and the world, he was a steadfast champion for human rights, the cause of peace and the care for the poor."

More than 12,000 filed into the Sacred Heart Basilica for the visitation to pay their respects and thousands more attended the wake service and funeral Mass. The plain silver coffin was taken by hearse to the cemetery where all Holy Cross priests are buried. Hesburgh was laid to rest under a simple cross, indistinguishable from the graves of other priests and brothers.

The following evening, more than 10,000 people filled the Purcell Pavilion at the Joyce Center to participate in a memorial tribute to Hesburgh. The speakers included former President Jimmy Carter, former First Lady Rosalynn, former U.S. Secretary of State Condoleezza Rice, Cardinal Theodore McCarrick of Washington, D.C., and former Notre Dame football coach Lou Holtz.

Hesburgh in a pre-recorded message got the last word, concluding the memorial service with a familiar Irish blessing.

"May the road rise up to meet you. May the wind be always at your back. May the sun shine warmly on your face. And may the rain fall soft upon your fields. And until we meet again, may God hold you in the very palm of his hand."

Resources:

Notre Dame Archives, Posted Oct. 7, 2011, "The Peace Corps and Notre Dame"

University of Notre Dame, Rev. Theodore M. Hesburgh, C.S.C.; contact Dennis Brown, Feb. 27, 2015

Scholastic, Notre Dame Student magazine, April 16, 2015, "Father Hesburgh"

John Lungren, Jr., Hesburgh of Notre Dame, Sheed & Ward, 1987.

CHAPTER THREE

Authorized for use by his administrative assistant, Maria Elena Bessignano
Father Gustavo Gutiérrez, O.P., is the author of "liberation theology" which gained favor among liberal clerics in Latin America, but not immediately by the Vatican.

"Poverty is the result of unjust and sinful social structures. It's not fate, it's a condition. It's not a misfortune, it's an injustice.
—Gustavo Gutiérrez

CHAPTER THREE

GUSTAVO GUTIÉRREZ

1928 –
Lima, Peru   1963

He grew up among the poor of Lima, Peru, a Native American of mixed Quechua descent, the indigenous peasants of the *altiplano*. And he dedicated his life lessons to give hope to the downtrodden.

Gustavo Gutiérrez overcame a physical handicap, osteomyletis, a severe bone infection that left him bedridden and bound to a wheelchair for most of his teenage years.

"The world I knew in my youth was a world of injustice and oppression against the poor," he said. "I came from a continent in which more than 60 percent of the population lived in a state of poverty, most of them in extreme poverty."

Lima was very rich, and then very poor in his day. Tens of thousands of Andean Indians, starving from benign neglect by the government, suddenly descended upon the capital, squatting in the foothills as well as forming impoverished pockets behind tall walls, hidden in upscale neighborhoods.

In the 1960s, Lima's slums were among the worst in the world.

When Gustavo's physical condition improved, he studied medicine, psychiatry and humanities, got involved in Catholic Action and embarked on a mission to discover theological answers to Christian doctrines. He then decided to enter the seminary and was ordained a priest in 1959.

He studied theology in Europe, in Belgium and France, under the guidance of such notable theologians as Yves Congar and Henri de Lubac and while there he also gained access to the theologians of the Second Vatican Council, including Karl Rahner and Hans Kung.

Gutierrez focused his studies on Latin American reality. He spent much of his life living and working among the poor and oppressed in Lima. His experiences affected his theological development. It was the foundation and driving force of what came to be known as "liberation theology."

In 1971, his groundbreaking work, "A Theology of Liberation: History, Politics, Salvation" was published.

Three years earlier, at the Latin American Bishops' conference in Medellín, Colombia, the Church's "preferential option for the poor" was endorsed. It later became a key element in liberation theology as well as the central tenet of the church's teaching. In 1979, the same bishops' gathering in Puebla, Mexico, underscored that teaching.

Liberation theology arose as a Catholic response to the Marxist movements that forged Latin America's military dictatorships in the 1960s and 1970s. It criticized the church's close relations, including often overt support, with the regimes.

If affirmed that, rather than just focusing on seeking salvation in the afterlife, Catholics should act in the here and now against unjust societies that breed poverty.

But while many Catholic missionaries throughout Latin America enthusiastically subscribed to the new theological approach, the hierarchy in Rome was much more cautious and later even became antagonistic toward liberation theology.

In September 1984, a special assembly of Peruvian bishops was summoned to Rome for the express purpose of condemning Gutiérrez. However, his colleagues held firm to his ideals.

Cardinal Joseph Ratzinger, as head of the Vatican's Congregation for the Doctrine of the Faith from 1981 to 2005 before becoming Pope Benedict XVI, issued official critiques of liberation theology in 1984 and again in 1986.

He took issue with some theologians who inappropriately mixed Marxist reaction of the global economic system with Catholic theology. He later condemned liberation theology for its "serious ideological deviations."

While Gutiérrez was never officially sanctioned by Ratzinger, other theologians who sided with him, including Brazilian Leonardo Boff, were.

During the pontificate of Pope John Paul II, a fierce anti-communist, several theologians were taken to task for espousing Marxist ideas. The pope went public with his concerns when he visited Nicaragua and admonished priests who had joined the Sandinista government.

Gutiérrez defended liberation theology as a Christian response to the conditions in which a great part of Latin American population live. He said the focus of the problem was sin manifested in an unjust social structure.

"It has arisen out of the experience of the poor, the oppressed, the wretched of the earth with whom I live each week," he said.

"The problem increases when one sees that among the poor there is an absence of recognition of their own human dignity and of their condition as daughters and sons of God," Gutiérrez said.

"Poverty is the result of unjust and sinful social structures," he added. "It's not fate, it's a condition; it's not a misfortune, it's an injustice."

Liberation, according to Gutiérrez, has three main dimensions.

First, it involves political and social liberation, the elimination of the immediate causes of poverty and injustice.

Second, liberation involves the emancipation of the poor, the marginalized, the downtrodden and the oppressed from "all those things that limit their capacity to develop themselves freely and in dignity."

Third, liberation theology involves liberation from selfishness and sin, a re-establishment of a relationship with God and with other people.

Poverty, Gutiérrez said, is not a result of fate or laziness. Rather it's due to structural injustices that privilege some while marginalizing others. "To be poor is to be insignificant," he said. "Poverty means an early and unjust death."

He believes that poverty is not inevitable. "Collectively the poor can organize and facilitate social change," he said. When Jesus said "Blessed are the poor," he didn't say "Blessed is poverty."

It's been a long struggle for the priest who stood his theological ground with the Vatican for more than four decades.

He was ordained a diocesan priest and served slum parishes in Lima before embarking on his quest in defense of the poor. In 1998, he joined the Order of Preachers, in part as admiration for the Dominican theologians he met while studying in France.

"I had personal contact with the scholarly work of Fathers Congar, Chenu and Schillebeeckx," he said. "I was attracted to their profound understanding of the intimate relationship that should exist between theology, spirituality and the actual preaching of the Gospel.

"Liberation theology shares the same conviction," he said.

"My subsequent research into the life of Bartolomé de Las Casas and his ardent defense of the poor also played an important role in my decision."

Fray Bartolomé was a 16th century Dominican missionary who served as the first bishop of Chiapas, Mexico in 1542. His wealthy family was associated with Christopher Columbus but he decried the horrors of the conquest and the colonization of the New World. He lobbied the Spanish monarchy for laws to end the corrupt *encomienda* system which legalized slavery.

While the Vatican was cool if not hostile to Gutiérrez's theology as revolutions, laced with communism, raged throughout Latin America, his writings and teachings reached audiences at universities throughout the Americas as well as in Europe. He also has authored more than a dozen books and has written hundreds of articles.

He was the principal professor at the Pontifical University of Peru. In 1993 he received the Legion of Honor by the French government for his tireless work for human dignity.

Since 2001, he has held the John Cardinal O'Hara Professorship of Theology at the University of Notre Dame.

In the fall of 2013, at the age of 85, Gutiérrez experienced a breakthrough in his relations with Rome over his lifelong efforts to steer the church toward a preferential option for the poor.

He met with Pope Francis, who had endorsed a "poor church for the poor." The meeting was arranged by Archbishop Gerhard Ludwig Mueller, prefect of the Congregation for the Doctrine of the Faith, the Vatican's doctrinal watchdog.

It was a remarkable about-face for a movement that swelled in popularity but was later stamped out by the conservative pontificates of John Paul II and his long-time doctrinal czar, Benedict XVI.

In 2012, Pope Benedict appointed Mueller as his successor to the Congregation of the Doctrine of the Faith, despite the fact that he was a well-known admirer of Gutiérrez. The move signaled a thaw in the tension between liberation theology and the Vatican, spurred by the end of the Cold War and the demise of Communist regimes.

With the election of Pope Francis, the first pope from Latin America, liberation theology could no longer "remain in the shadows to which it has been relegated for years," according to the Vatican's newspaper, *L'Osservatore Romano.*

Mueller joined Gutiérrez in writing a book in 2004 but it didn't attract attention until 2013 when its Italian translation came out. In the book, Mueller describes liberation theology as one of the "most significant currents of Catholic theology of the 20th century." He added that it helped the church bridge the divide between "earthly happiness and ultra-earthly salvation."

Michael Lee, theology professor at Fordham University and a colleague of Gutiérrez, said the election of the Argentine pope brought an openness to liberation theology. "The reality of the Latin American experience is present in the person of Francis and in the Vatican now in a way that it has never been before."

He added, "It's a recognition that liberation theology and the kind of Christian action it inspired, and that fed it, is something very valuable and something our world needs today."

Paul Farmer, the U.S. physician and Harvard professor, known widely for his humanitarian health care work in Haiti and elsewhere in the Third World, said he was inspired by liberation theology. He recently co-authored a book with Gutiérrez entitled "In the Company of the Poor."

Farmer was encouraged by Pope Francis' meeting with Gutiérrez. "I hope it means an easing in the Vatican's stance toward liberation theology."

He'd like to see agencies, non-profit groups and governments that provide assistance to the world's most impoverished people adopt Gutierrez's "preferential option for the poor" and his work on issues of structural violence.

"If you don't understand structural violence," Farmer said, "you're grasping around in the dark in public health, public education and poverty reduction.

"These ideas warrant not just rehabilitation but widespread dissemination."

Gutiérrez, who celebrated his 87th birthday in 2015, remains optimistic that his lifetime work will bear fruit. "I hope my life tries to give testimony to the message of the Gospel, above all that God loves the world and He loves those who are the poorest within it."

Resources:

John Deer, S.J., National Catholic Reporter, "Preferential Option for the Poor"; Nov. 8, 2007.

Joshua McElwee, The Independent News Source, "Pope Meets Liberation Theology Pioneer," Sept. 25, 2013.

Daniel Hartnett, S.J., America, "Remembering the Poor," Feb. 3, 2003.

Alessandro Speciale, Religion News Service, "Pope Francis to meet Gutierrez,' Sept. 10, 2013.

CHAPTER FOUR

Photo by Peter A. Geniesse

Father Leo Mahon in 1965 constructed an "experimental cathedral" at his parish, Cristo Redentor, in San Miguelito, Panama, along with five satellite church stations, with funds from the Chicago archdiocese.

"The institutional church was no more willing to allow an experimental structure to thrive within itself than was the government to allow a democratic society."
–Leo Mahon

CHAPTER FOUR

LEO MAHON'S 'EXPERIMENT'

1926-2013
San Miguelito, Panama,   1965

It was a noble experiment.

A young priest moves into an unchurched slum in Panama, gathers in a few disciples -- sinners all -- empowers them with the Spirit and creates a remarkable Christian community.

It's the story of Leo Thomas Mahon, an Irish lad who grew up on Chicago's West Side. His father was a policeman, but at age 13, Leo wanted to be a missionary. At age 34 he got his wish.

Chicago's Cardinal Albert Meyer was mulling his church's role in Pope John XXIII's call to assist the priest-poor nations of Latin America. A nondescript barrio of San Miguelito, a sprawling suburb of Panama City, came to the forefront.

But Meyer wasn't about to send three of his best young priests without a plan. The challenge ahead was to establish an "experimental" parish, an uncharted mission to serve the unserved.

Father Leo had worked with Puerto Ricans at Holy Cross Parish, and was director of the Cardinal's Committee for the Spanish Speaking. He formed a parish leadership team among the Puerto Ricans and Mexicans who were coming to Chicago in droves. He called it *"Hermanos en la Familia de Dios,"* and before long it counted 300 men. Since the Hispanic culture was one of male domination, only men needed apply.

31

When Cardinal Meyer returned from an official trip to Rome, he called Mahon in his office and asked him to put together a full-scale plan for an archdiocesan mission in Panama. Father Leo would head the project and he could choose his running mates: Fathers Jack Greeley and Bob McGlinn. The three arrived in Panama on a freight vessel carrying a Nicaraguan flag on Feb. 22, 1963.

Mahon had submitted several alternatives for administering the mission. Cardinal Meyer gave the go-ahead for an "experimental" parish plan. He saw its potential as a valuable training ground for Chicago priests who were to be assigned to Spanish-speaking parishes.

The three priests were welcomed into San Miguelito without fanfare. The parish church was a rickety shed, made of old boards and topped by a tin roof. Their first mass was attended by some children, five women and one old man. After the service, they encountered four men playing dominoes nearby who challenged the priests' intentions.

"Why did you come here?" one shouted.

"To start a revolution," Father Leo said.

That was a conversation starter over six-packs of beer that went on into the night and created a friendship that would last for years. They talked of the poverty in San Miguelito, and the lack of water and sewers, roads and schools, a cinema and even a police station.

Father Leo saw it as an opportunity for community organizing. He recalled how Saul Alinsky did it among the poor of South Chicago. "He taught us to organize on the felt needs of the people," he said. "There were so many needs in San Miguelito. We had so much to organize."

He started a new parish group called *Los Hombres Cristianos de San Miguelito*. It was open to men only. That concept was challenged by a group of women who said, "Our men are not to be trusted." One woman added, "They booze and whore and sleep their days away. They don't respect themselves or us."

Father Leo asked for a year to work with just the men, and the women reluctantly concurred. The three priests pounded on doors, talked to men about problems and priorities and in a short time there were 400 men organized and divided into committees. They worked in the fields of education, *"Caritas,"* construction, youth and finance.

Before the year was up, the parish was becoming a living Christian community. A series of 12-week religion courses had drawn 600 people. It was time to recruit and train lay leaders. Father Leo invited 30 men to be adult catechists, Christian community organizers. They were designated as lay deacons. They were to run the *Familia de Dios* programs, and serve as lectors and commentators at masses.

That October, the parish held a mission on the campus of Colegio Belén on three successive Sundays. The first Sunday was for youths 15-21 and was attended by 350. The second Sunday was for men and 250 showed up. The last mission was for women, which drew 350. Cursillos were offered and 70 signed up at the start.

The numbers continued to grow. Palm Sunday processions at five different areas of the parish drew 2,100 and Good Friday attracted 3,000. Ten chapels were in the planning stages to further decentralize the parish and a large parish center, designed to accommodate 1,000 people was under construction.

The region was growing, too. In 1963 San Miguelito had a population of 25,000. A dozen years later, it had soared to 200,000

Father Leo's experiment was succeeding and the word had spread through Panama and beyond. He was invited to speak about his "experiment" throughout Central America, in Peru and Brazil and in Chile which was hosting the annual South American Catholic Church conference.

The native clergy, at first, were hostile to the changes. Their churches were accustomed to charging for the sacraments. San Miguelito would have none of that. Their churches distributed U.S. surplus food to the poor through "*Caritas*," an arm of Catholic Relief Services, but Father Leo said no. He didn't want to be seen as an "agent for the colossus of the North."

The native priests also were upset by the construction of his "cathedral," Cristo Redentor in San Miguelito, a circular structure built like a huge tent with no pillars and open sides to catch the cooling breezes. It wasn't the structure. Rather it was the mural behind the altar that was dedicated to liberation of the poor. The clergy were depicted as severe figures garbed in black, holding a cross above their heads in their right hand while grasping money with their left.

That didn't bother Panama's Archbishop Tomas Clavel, however, who had taken great interest in the San Miguelito project. When one of his native priests stated at a conference, "Monseñor, what you really want is for us to be like the priests of San Miguelito," Clavel responded, "Yes, that's what I want." A few years later, Clavel was forced to resign.

A Passion Play was put on during Lent, with a local flair. Jesus was a peasant who didn't die on the cross but rather as the result of gunshots fired by a hired assassin. The soldiers were not Roman but rather from the *Guardia Nacional.* Thousands came to see the production, including the president of the Republic, accompanied by cabinet ministers and flanked by bodyguards from the *Guardia Nacional.*

On Good Friday, the streets and hills of San Miguelito were lined with 70 crosses and the multiple processions drew more than five thousand people. At each of the 14 stations of the Cross, men delivered meditations on the suffering and evil in their own lives and in society.

Father Leo was pleased with the public demonstrations and the new-found faith of his parishioners. But he still was upset that nothing was being done to curb the corrupted political power in Panama. He had 30 dedicated lay deacons, three priests and five Maryknoll nuns, who had recently arrived. "We were making a significant difference in the personal lives of the men, women and children of San Miguelito," he said. "But encircling us every day was the heavy arm of dictatorship and corruption."

He said that one of the threats that encouraged him to get involved in politics was the fear of communism taking over the country. Both the Communist Party and communist propaganda were outlawed but he noted that the situation was ripe with the lack of jobs, poor distribution of wealth and ineffective and often corrupt government.

Also to blame, he underscored the lack of clearly enunciated Christian revolutionary principles and a shortage of trained Christian organizers, both lay and clerical.

Father Leo sent periodic reports of the experiment to Chicago's Cardinal Meyer, who heartily endorsed his approach. "There seems to be a new way, a new church coming out of communities like San Miguelito," Meyer said. "So please keep going. I want our young priests to catch that spirit."

At first Meyer offered to send as much as half of the newly ordained priests to spend a year in training at the mission. Father Leo settled on three additional priests from the archdiocese.

Cardinal Meyer never got to see the dedication of Cristo Redentor in San Miguelito. He died suddenly of a brain tumor. Father Leo returned to Chicago for the funeral and to say goodbye to his friend and patron. Meyer's successor was John Patrick Cody, the archbishop of New Orleans.

At first, Cardinal Cody wasn't too enthusiastic about inheriting an archdiocesan mission in Panama. That was before he decided to visit San Miguelito. After an enthusiastic reception by parishioners, the cardinal said he was ready to move in when he retired – if the guest lodging were a bit more engaging.

Cody pledged his support of the mission. "Leo, we will give you what you need," he said. "Send me a proposal. Chicago will make it happen." By 1966, he had made good on his promise. He financed the construction of five parish churches, each one costing $85,000.

Father Leo was anxious to decentralize his parish. There now were five priests and five nuns and 30 lay deacons, plus hundreds of committed Christian leaders, many who had completed Cursillos, in the experiment that was just three years old. A priest and a sister were assigned as co-pastors of each parish station. Padre León, as he was known, remained at Cristo Redentor, the initial central parish on the hill, along with co-pastor Madre Cecilia.

He introduced the Christian Family Movement, and Young Christian Workers, Catholic action concepts developed in Belgium. In each of the five parishes there were as many as 20 groups of eight to ten persons. Leader couples became the hub of planning for their sectors.

San Miguelito not only was a highly successful experimental Christian community, it also had become a political force to be reckoned with. President Arnulfo Arias and his party *Panamanista,* were heavy favorites in the community – that is until he was overthrown in a coup in 1968. A group of men, involved in a parish political action committee called "Mundo," saw an opportunity to foster democracy and curb corruption throughout the country.

They sent a manifesto to the military junta demanding a guarantee of civil rights, free elections, a prompt return to civilian rule and above all, fair representation for the people of San Miguelito. They pledged that if their manifesto was ignored, they would organize a protest march against the "temporary" government.

On Oct. 23, 1968, 50 marchers soon became 500 and they walked, six abreast with arms locked, down the hill, carrying a large wooden cross and praying the *Padre Nuestro*. As they neared a rise in the street they encountered a battalion of National Guardsmen with tear gas canisters and machine guns. The commander strode up to Padre León, dressed in his white cassock, and shouted in his face, "Go back where you came from. You will not pass."

The major decided to check in with his boss, Colonel Omar Torrijos, a sometime acquaintance of Padre León. He then announced that Torrijos had given permission for the march to continue "on one condition: that you allow us to escort you in order to prevent any violence."

The crowds roared their approval, and joined the marchers who were bracketed by the soldiers. By the time they had arrived at the church in Villa Guadalupe, the protesters numbered five thousand.

Still, the junta refused to respond to the manifesto. As the "Mundo" leaders prepared for another march, Padre León was called to Army Headquarters to meet with Colonel Torrijos.

"You won yesterday," Torrijos roared. "But you'll never make fools of us again." He continued, "We have risked our lives, our careers and our families on the coup and we're not going to let someone like you take it all away."

Panama's future dictator ranted on. "Your life right now is not worth one cent. We're not afraid to kill if we have to," he said, adding "I could have you put on a plane and flown to the States tonight."

Then he calmed down and turned to Padre León. "Do you know that if every part of Panama did what you people have done, we could not control this country?"

Padre León nodded and said, "Yes, that's just the point of it all."

Shortly thereafter, Torrijos assumed the rank of general and became the chief of the army and ruler of the nation. He tried to mend fences with Padre León and the parish leaders, saying that he was impressed with the movement in San Miguelito. He even promoted the community as the "model city" of Panama.

That Christmas a young Guardia handed Padre León an envelope that contained 20 hundred dollar bills. *"Felices Pascuas, Padre,* a gift from the general." The priest distributed the money to the poor in his parish, $50 for each family.

The General Assembly elections took place without the usual irregularities, violence, and buying votes with liquor. In fact, 53 of the seats in the Assembly were won by persons who had taken part in the parish's evangelization programs. "Panamanian history had been made," Padre León said.

He had an appointment with Cardinal Cody in Chicago to report on the happenings in San Miguelito. Instead, Cody suggested Padre León change careers, and take over a parish in Chicago.

Padre León turned to his friend, Panama Archbishop Marcos McGrath, C.S.C., for counsel. "I received a request from the government to remove you from Panama," McGrath said. When he declined, the regime made the same request to the Vatican, "and that's how the matter got to Cardinal Cody."

Padre León wasn't ready to leave his experiment, and Cardinal Cody wasn't about to order his return to the U.S. He said if the Vatican wanted him transferred, the Vatican would have to do it.

Padre León was leaving his mark on the community and not everyone was pleased. The native clergy had grown restless over the Chicago priest who wouldn't follow their lead. Torrijos and his cabinet were growing weary meeting the challenges he constantly presented. And Rome was uneasy about the experiment, fearing liberation theology was making inroads in Panama. They all wanted him gone.

The issue came to a head when the Panamanian bishops leveled charges of misconduct and heresy against him. The charges were summarily dismissed after an inquisition that was more about control, Padre León said. "They were in control, or at least they thought they should be, and my not being under control was the real offense."

Earlier, he had been appointed episcopal vicar by Archbishop Clavel. It was a new post-Vatican II position conferred on a priest, extending him many powers of a bishop. The designation made him responsible for the largest portion of the Archdiocese of Panama, with a Catholic population nearing 200,000. But that position wasn't enough to fend off his growing opposition.

The papal nuncio for Panama delivered the dagger. The Vatican had formed a commission to again investigate San Miguelito. It would be comprised of five cardinals and the master general of the Dominicans. He was never informed of their conclusions.

"Late in the year 1974, I found myself with not really enough energy or spirit to do justice to my increased responsibilities," he said. "The government of Panama harried me at every opportunity. Each time I left the country I feared I would not be allowed to return.

"Slowly the decision came into focus: I would have to leave Panama," he said. "The forces arrayed against us were too powerful." He added, "The institutional church was no more willing to allow an experimental structure to thrive within itself than was the government to allow a democratic society."

The mission continued without Father Leo for a few years, but as the forces against the priests tightened, they returned to the States, unable to feel safe or needed.

Pope John Paul II appointed Vasquez Pinto to replace Father Leo as episcopal vicar. He was directed to get rid of anything that "reeked of liberation theology." He fired the lay leaders in all the parishes and forbade them to minister. He prohibited any practice that would represent the essence of what Cardinal Meyer had begun – building an experimental church.

For the next 30 years, Father Leo served two large congregations in the Chicago Archdiocese, St. Victor's in Calumet City and St. Mary of the Woods on Chicago's north side. He became a pastor emeritus in 2005 and he died at age 87 on May 20, 2013.

I first met Father Leo Mahon at Cuernavaca, Mexico, in the summer of 1963, just a few months after he had established his mission at San Miguelito, Panama. Msgr. Ivan Illich invited him to stay a week at CIDOC so he could pick his brains about plans for his "experimental" parish. Illich also wanted his center's residents, lay and religious, to open their minds to a new approach to mission before they headed to their assignments.

Father Leo was excited to share his dreams with future missionaries, presenting seminars in the afternoons and give-and-take sessions in the evening over Cuba Libres and shots of tequila. He invited the participants to check out his parish on their way down south. I did just that.

Father Ray Zagorski, the Green Bay Diocesan director for PAVLA, joined me for a flying mission tour that included stops at Guatemala City, Panama City, Bogotá, Lima, and Santiago. Our intent was to assess the American missions, and report our findings to Father Fernandez, then national director of the Papal Volunteers for Latin America.

The Maryknoll missions in the interior of Guatemala got good grades. So did the Norbertines in Lima. But San Miguelito certainly scored the highest. Not so with Bogotá or Santiago where many PAVLA volunteers were not being put to good use.

In some cases, volunteers were seen as cheap help and there was no mission to the poor. Nurses generally were productive in rural and slum districts, but teachers often served the upper class, teaching English in Catholic schools. The program had little oversight. The bishops put in an order for volunteers, they arrived and they were on their own, for better or worse.

When my tour of duty in northern Chile ended in the fall of 1965, I flew into Panama to visit Father Mahon and to check up on his experiment. I was stunned by the physical and organizational changes at San Miguelito, and I was heartened by the role the laity was playing in the Christian community. It was right out of the Second Vatican Council.

Years later, as I followed the experiment in the news, I became dismayed at the Catholic Church's sanctioning of Father Mahon for establishing a Christian community known throughout the world as a model of faith, justice and peace.

Sources:

Leo Mahon and Nancy Davis: "Fire Under My Feet," A memoir of God's Power in Panama; Orbis Books, 2007.

Archdiocese of Chicago: Obituaries, Msgr. Leo T. Mahon; May 22, 2013

CHAPTER FIVE

Photo by Peter A. Geniesse
Decades after his death in 1973, Chile installed a statue of Salvador Allende in the presidents' row in front of *La Moneda* in downtown Santiago. The plaque reads: "I have faith in Chile and its destiny."

"Never before has Chile had a more democratic government than that over which I have the honor to preside."
—Salvador Allende

CHAPTER FIVE

CHILE'S SALVADOR ALLENDE

1908-1973
Antofagasta, Chile   1964

"Allende, Allende, Allende *me defiende.*"

The chant grew louder and louder as thousands descended from their hovels on the hill to Plaza Colon where Salvador Allende was awaiting their praises. The perennial socialist candidate, who once served as the region's senator, scored well with the desert dwellers in his previous two campaigns for president of Chile. But it was a different story with the voters of the south, Santiago, Valparaiso and Viña del Mar.

However, this time Allende had a good chance of becoming the first Marxist to be freely elected president of a country.

The crowd, dominated by the poor from the *poblaciones,* was energized by that prospect. They had followed his political career and believed in the promises of the physician from Santiago. It seemed that no one else in the nation's capital cared for the people of the desert. Antofagasta was so far north that to southerners it was more Bolivian than Chilean.

In fact, the province did belong to Bolivia until the War of the Pacific in 1874.

The North, home to the Atacama Desert, the driest on earth, was natural resource rich. Its mines paid most of Chile's bills for more than a century. But the *Norteños* never got the respect they had earned.

For more than 60 years, nitrate ruled the land. There were 170 *oficinas salitreras* in the desert, company-owned towns on the *pampa*. Thousands of workers were employed and housed alongside the surface mines. It was a hard life for families, isolated in the dusty desert with daytime temperatures reaching 100 and nights below freezing.

But it was a job, and the mining revenues accounted for half of Chile's gross national product. Freighters from all over the world docked in the Antofagasta harbor to load tons of nitrate, also known as saltpeter, to be converted into agricultural fertilizer. The concentration of nitrates in the desert, and nary a drop of rain, ruled out any vegetation. However, Antofagasta's main boulevard grew grass, flowers and palm trees, thanks to the soil brought in as ballast in the holds of foreign ships.

At the turn of the 20th century, synthetic nitrate was developed in Germany, spelling disaster for Chile's industry. The mining boom came to an abrupt halt at the end of the 1930s. More than 150 *oficinas salitreras* suddenly became ghost towns. Everyone left, and everything was left behind. No one could live on the *pampa* without a water source.

Thousands of workers and their families, without paychecks or pensions, flocked to the sandy slopes of the *Cordillera de la Costa*, high above Antofagasta, forming a shantytown of tin and cardboard huts, without electricity, sewers or water. They were abandoned, but they weren't invisible. They had a clear view of downtown Antofagasta, nestled on the shores of the Pacific Ocean. And their shacks served as a stark everyday reminder to the well-off that there were poor in their midst.

Some of the miners went to work in the sea. The Humboldt Current is what makes the Atacama Desert the driest place on the globe. The marine air is cooled by the current, curbing precipitation onshore. The Humboldt also is a fisherman's delight, when El Niño cooperates, as it draws billions upon billions of anchovies and sardines onto the offshore shelf and creates an extraordinary abundance of marine life.

Trawlers haul tons of the tiny fish to numerous processing plants along the northern coast of Chile where they are turned into animal food – and fertilizer.

Some of the nitrate miners later moved to Chuquicamata, about 130 miles northwest of Antofagasta, the site of the world's largest open-pit copper mine. It was owned and operated by Anaconda Copper Mining Company. The U.S. industrial behemoth purchased the mine for $77 million in 1922. "Chuqui" netted Anaconda $111 million in 1956 alone, yielding two-thirds of the company's total profits that year.

Most of the former nitrate miners, however, remained unemployed or under-employed. Some were disabled with lung diseases. There was no insurance, no workman's compensation, no pension, no settlements. They felt abandoned by their government and by its leaders 700 miles to the south.

But they did have faith in Allende. He had pledged to speak for the downtrodden and for more than three decades in public office he had consistently voted on the side of the worker.

"Allende, Allende, Allende, *me defiende.*"

Even the teenagers had taken up the chant as Allende stepped onto the podium in the city square. It wasn't just a slogan, but a commitment of trust. Their parents had voted for Allende in the 1952 presidential elections, and again six years later when he was the *Frente de Accion Popular* candidate. In 1958 he tallied 28 percent of the vote. Jorge Alessandri won with just 31 percent. The stage was set for 1964.

Allende warmed up his audience by announcing that when he became president he would nationalize the "Chuqui" mine. A roar went up from the crowd. They waved their signs and placards with anti-American political slogans. The United States was symbolized by an octopus named Uncle Sam with its tentacles snatching *escudos* and bars of copper and choking Chile off the map.

Other presidential candidates had called for the nationalization of all foreign owned copper mines in the past, but it was mostly political talk. Allende would make it happen,

Anaconda and Kennecott, two giant U.S. corporations, controlled both copper production and Chile's economy. The people on the *pampa* were reminded of that every day as they watched long freight trains laden with tons of copper bars arrive at the docks in Antofagasta to be loaded on ships heading to the United States.

Allende's campaign stop drew more than 500,000, if one were to believe the Communist daily, or less than 5,000 if one preferred the right-wing daily. Chile had six national daily newspapers, one for each of the political parties, and they shaded the news and facts to the likes of their subscribers.

I joined a number of journalists near the platform where Allende was speaking. We concluded that the number was probably closer to 20,000.

As I walked among the crowds in Plaza Colon in front of the Catholic cathedral, I noticed a large poster display singing the praises of *Alianza para el Progreso,* the United States' program for aid to Latin America. Included was a huge photo of President John F. Kennedy, who was assassinated on Nov. 22, 1963, just three months earlier.

As Allende continued to lambast the U.S. for its flawed foreign policies, there were tears in the eyes of those who circled about the display and JFK's giant photo, oblivious to his ranting message.

Chileans, like most Latin Americans, loved Kennedy. On the day he died, all Chilean flags were at half-staff, the radio stations played only somber classical music and everywhere I went I was greeted with *abrazos* and expressions of sympathy for "our president."

When I returned to my *pensionado* the evening of the political rally, I was bombarded with questions from two roommates who were leaders in the local Communist Party. They wanted to know what I thought of Allende's address, and my reaction to his call for the nationalization of the copper mines.

"First," I said, "I'd like to know what you think of President Kennedy."

"I would have voted for him," Pedro said. "Me, too," Ernesto said.

Allende didn't win the presidency that time around, making it three straight defeats. He did have a plurality in the Province of Antofagasta, however, and it was his best showing overall with 38 per cent of the votes. Christian Democrat Eduardo Frei was elected with 55 per cent, including brokered votes from Radical Party candidate Julio Duran who saw Frei as the "lesser of two evils."

Allende, a veteran politico with more than three decades in public office, wasn't crestfallen by his defeat. Rather, he remarked in gest that his epitaph should say, "Here lies the next president of Chile."

In 1970, he again was on the ballot. His political positions were no secret. He was the founder of the Socialist Party of Chile way back in 1933 and through the years he had fostered a number of progressive social programs, including universal health care in the 1950s, the first such program in the Americas. Among other legislation he steered included safety laws protecting workers, pensions for widows, maternity care and free lunch for school children.

On his fourth try, as the leader of *Unidad Popular*, with a nod from the Chilean Communist Party in case its candidate, world-reknowned poet Pablo Neruda bowed out, Allende, at age 62, won the presidency with 36 per cent of the vote. He edged his familiar rival and former president Jorge Alessandri, who had 35 percent. The third candidate, Radomiro Tomic, of the Christian Democratic Party, tallied 27 per cent.

The Chilean Constitution called for Congress, in the event of no majority winner, to pick one from the top two candidates. Tradition favored the top vote getter. After all, Alessandri was elected with just 31 per cent of the popular vote back in 1958, in defeating Allende.

One month later, the Senate still had not ruled a victor, and things got out of control. Gen. Rene Schneider, commander in chief of the army and defender of the "constitutionalist doctrine," was shot resisting a kidnaping attempt by a group headed by rival Gen. Roberto Viaux.

Viaux's scheme had been supported by the United States CIA on orders from President Richard Nixon to do whatever was necessary "to get rid of him," referring to Allende. The Senate, stung by the Schneider's death, voted to put Allende in office two days later.

Allende assumed the presidency on Nov. 3, 1970, signed "The Statute of Constitutional Guarantees" to gain support from the Christian Democrats and immediately went to work on his "Chilean Path to Socialism." Former President Frei and his Christian Democrats already had set the stage for massive social change in Chile, and their political platform was not unlike Allende's.

In Allende's first two years in office, Chile nationalized the copper industries and banking institutions, took over the health care and educational systems, eliminated the *Latifundia* which limited all estates to less than 80 hectares, raised wages and cut taxes for the middle class, built 120,000 houses for the homeless, granted amnesty for political prisoners and restored diplomatic relations with Cuba.

The rate of inflation fell and real wages rose by 22 percent in the first year. Price controls were instituted, literacy programs were launched, and "Allendistas" traveled into the countryside and shanty towns to perform volunteer work. Allende was off to a good start.

However, in late 1972 the rising economy soured, in part due to the U.S. campaign against the Allende government. The Chilean *escudo* hit an inflation rate of 140 percent. The combination of inflation and government-mandated price-fixing, together with the disappearance of basic commodities from supermarket shelves led to the rise in black markets for rice, beans, sugar and flour.

That October the first of a wave of strikes was led by truckers and later by small businessmen, professional unions and students. Export income fell due to a severe drop in the price of copper on international markets. Copper represented more than half of Chile's export receipts, and the price suddenly had been cut by a third. Also, when Chile nationalized its copper industry, the U.S. cut off its credits and increased its support of opposition leaders.

Allende's bold socialist policies, combined with his close ties to Cuba, heightened fears in Washington. The Nixon administration continued to exert economic pressure on Chile via multilateral organizations. Immediately after his election, Nixon directed the CIA and U.S. State Department officials to "put pressure" on the Allende government. He even went further by authorizing $10 million to stop Allende from coming into power or on a campaign to unseat him.

Allende's election was deemed a disaster by a U.S. administration that wanted to prevent the spread of Communism during the Cold War. U.S. Secretary of State Henry Kissinger's 40 Committee and the CIA came up with elaborate schemes to impede Allende from taking office.

Throughout his presidency, Allende remained at odds with the Chilean Congress, which was dominated by the Christian Democratic Party. Allende and his opponents in Congress repeatedly accused each other of undermining the Chilean Constitution.

On June 29, 1973, tanks surrounded the presidential palace in a failed coup by the nationalist paramilitary group, *Patria y Libertad*. A general strike at the end of July included the copper miners at El Teniente. In August, the Supreme Court of Chile publicly complained about the inability of the Allende government to enforce the law of the land.

On August 22, the Chamber of Deputies, by a vote of 81 to 47, passed a resolution accusing Allende of a laundry list of constitutional offenses, claiming the president had a goal of establishing a "totalitarian system." Allende countered by accusing Congress of promoting a *coup d'etat* or a civil war.

"Chilean democracy is a conquest by all the people," he wrote in response. "Never before has Chile had a more democratic government than that over which I have the honor to preside."

That same day, Gen. Carlos Prats resigned as defense minister and commander in chief of the army. Allende replaced him with Gen. Augusto Pinochet, who once commanded the 1st Army division, based in Antofagasta.

In early September, Allende proposed a plebiscite in an effort to resolve the constitutional crisis. His speech outlining the details was scheduled to be presented Sept. 11. He never had a chance to deliver it.

On Sept. 11, 1973, the combined Chilean armed forces overthrew Allende's government in a coup during which the presidential palace, *La Moneda*, was strafed and shelled. The president, a prisoner in his own office, gave his farewell speech on the radio amid increasing gunfire and explosions. He spoke of his great love for Chile and of his deep faith in its future.

And then he died of a self-inflicted gunshot wound.

Resources:

Salvador Allende: Wikipedia, the free encyclopedia; as of April 6, 2015

BBC News: Profile Salvador Allende, Sept. 8, 2003.

New York Times: Salvador Allende, last updated Oct. 8, 2015.

Encyclopaedia Britanica: President of Chile.

Mining Technology: Chuquicamata Copper Mine.

CHAPTER SIX

Photo by Peter A. Geniesse

A "carbineri" guards La Moneda, Chile's presidential palace, where Gen. Augusto Pinochet ordered the siege and assassination of President Salvador Allende on Sept. 11, 1973. After the bloody coup, Pinochet installed himself as president-dictator until 1990.

"Drastic measures were necessary to save the country from communism. I take political responsibility for everything that was done."
–Augusto Pinochet

CHAPTER SIX

GEN. AUGUSTO PINOCHET

1915-2006
Santiago, Chile   1973

Back in the 1960s, there was a popular paperback in Spanish making the rounds in Chile. It was entitled *"Revolución en Chile"* by Sillie Utternut. It was all fictitious, a message just for laughs. It told a tale about a *"gringa"* journalist from Michigan who got wind of a political uprising in Santiago. She traveled to Chile to get a "scoop" on the story and she clumsily created a scene of chaos.

The subliminal message, if indeed there was one, was that Chile wasn't like its Latin American neighbors which went from coup to coup, junta to junta, and from dictator to dictator, often with the assistance of the United States.

No one with any sense of Latin American history would ever think that democratic Chile would succumb to a government *coup d'etat*. Countries like Argentina, Bolivia, Peru and Brazil, along with the "Banana Republics" seemed to change their leadership every fortnight.

Chileans looked down their noses at their neighbors' politics. Santiago had a cosmopolitan, European feel, and most Chileans did come from Europe, or somewhere else. The country was mature, tolerant, sophisticated and above all a paragon of democracy.

And then along came Gen. Augusto Pinochet.

Less than one month after President Salvador Allende appointed Pinochet commander-in-chief of the army, Pinochet led the combined Chilean Armed Forces (Army, Navy, Air Force and *Carabineros*) in an all-out assault on *La Moneda*, the presidential palace, to oust his *patrón*.

The date was Sept. 11, 1973. Air Force planes attacked the palace with rockets and bombs and tanks opened fire after Allende rejected an initial demand for his resignation. The president then asked for a five-minute ceasefire in order to resign. His plea was rejected.

Troops blasted buildings in the city center and helicopters machine-gunned the top floors of buildings near the British Embassy in downtown Santiago. At least 17 bombs were dropped on the presidential palace.

Most authorities agree that Allende committed suicide rather than surrender. However, some still insist he was assassinated.

The purge of dissidents, communists and socialists and just plain political opponents was about to begin. That first year some 3,200 were executed, 30,000 were tortured and 80,000 were interned. About 1,000 are still missing.

Thousands of Chilean citizens were rounded up and detained in Santiago's soccer stadium where many of the executions occurred. Thousands more were shipped to isolated sites throughout the country.

In 1971, President Allende declared that Chacabuco, an abandoned nitrate town in the Atacama Desert, not far from Antofagasta, was an Historic Monument of Chile. Two years later, Pinochet turned that monument into a concentration camp for 1,800 prisoners. Security was enforced by a ring of 100 landmines around the site. Many of the detained were never heard from again.

A total of 1,312 citizens were exiled, and they weren't even safe in foreign lands. Gen. Carlos Prats, the army commander under Allende, was assassinated in Buenos Aires, Argentina, and Orlando Letalier, former Chilean ambassador to the U.S., was killed in Washington, D.C. by a car bomb. They were among 119 opponents who were killed in "Operation Condor," a multi-national, anti-communism campaign orchestrated by the United States' CIA. In October 1973 another 70 people were slain throughout the country by the "Caravan of Death."

Pinochet, the leading plotter of the coup, said the drastic measures were necessary "to save the country from communism."

There is no evidence that the U.S. was directly involved in the coup. However, the CIA did play a key role in the three-year conspiracy against the Allende government. The U.S. imposed an invisible blockade that was designed to disrupt the economy and contribute to the destabilization of the regime.

The U.S. provided material support to the military government after the coup, and put some of Pinochet's officers on the CIA payroll, even though they were known to be involved in human rights abuses.

A four-man military junta was established immediately after the coup. The Constitution and Congress were suspended, strict censorship and a curfew were imposed, all parties were banned and all political activities were halted. On Dec. 17, 1974 the junta turned over the executive powers to Pinochet, granting him the title of president.

That year Pinochet created the Directorate of National Intelligence, or DINA, a fear-inspiring secret police agency which took part in a number of high-profile murders beyond Chile's borders.

Pinochet called for a plebiscite on Sept. 11, 1980, to ratify a new constitution, replacing the one adopted in 1925. It gave almost unlimited powers to the presidency. It created the Constitutional Tribunal and the controversial National Security Council and extended the presidential term to eight years, allowing the junta to pick the successor.

Pinochet had little use for political parties, banning all of them. He blamed the democratic political system for having allowed a coalition of Socialists and Communists to take control of the government. He said he was against Communism as well as "orthodox democracy," which he claimed was "too easy to infiltrate and destroy."

After the coup he insisted that Chile would require "an authoritarian government that has the capacity to act decisively."

He appointed military officers as mayors of towns and cities throughout Chile. Retired military personnel were named rectors of universities, and they carried out purges of faculty members suspected of left-wing or liberal sympathies.

In 1986, the U.S. government was so worried that left-wing opposition might erupt into a civil war that it considered offering asylum to Chile's president. Ronald Reagan reportedly admired Pinochet and wanted to go to Chile "to personally thank him for saving the country and to tell him it was time to go."

But George Schulz, U.S. Secretary of State, said no way, adding that Pinochet had "too much blood on his hands."

Pinochet called for a second plebiscite in 1988, believing the people would back him for another eight years as president. However, 56 percent of the people voted against him. He ignored the results and continued in office until 1990, serving a total of 17 years as president-dictator. He held on to his post as commander-in-chief of the army until 1997 when he became "Senator for Life."

He resigned as senator in 2002, claiming mild dementia and physical infirmities, ailments that had him avoid trials in hundreds of court cases. Four years earlier, while he was recuperating from a back operation in a London clinic, he was arrested by British police in response to a Spanish judge seeking Pinochet's extradition to Madrid to stand trial on charges of genocide, torture and kidnapping of Spanish citizens.

After 16 months of legal battles, he was deemed physically unfit to stand trial in Spain and he was sent back to Chile to face more charges. By the time of his death on Dec. 10, 2006, at age 91, he was facing more than 300 criminal charges for human rights violations.

The National Commission on Truth and Reconciliation later cited 3,200 victims by name and described the ghastly circumstances of their deaths by firing squads, beatings, mutilations, drownings and electrocutions, all attributed to Pinochet's security forces.

Investigators also said that Pinochet had $28 million in secret bank accounts in several countries. Later they discovered 10 tons of gold, valued at $160 million, in Pinochet's name in a Hong Kong bank.

The 17-year Chilean nightmare was over in the year 2000 when Ricardo Lagos, the first Socialist to be elected since the overthrow of Allende, assumed the presidency.

"There is one consensus today shared by everyone," Lagos said during his inauguration. "Never again! Never again can Chile repeat that which ruptured Chile's soul. Never again!"

Six years later, Lagos was succeeded by another Socialist, Michelle Bachelet, a former political prisoner who was exiled. Her father, an Air Force general loyal to Allende, was jailed by his colleagues, tortured and died in prison.

Why did millions of Chileans continue to support a dictator for 17 years when they knew he was responsible for the execution of thousands of their countrymen? To most of the world, he was declared a pariah. He didn't squirm, or dodge the blame. "I take political responsibility for everything that was done," he said on the occasion of his 91st birthday.

In 2004, I returned to Chile after nearly 40 years and spent several days in Santiago with a friend of a friend, a retired wealthy businessman who sang the praises of Pinochet.

"He saved us from communism," he said. "He did what was necessary. Besides, all that stuff that they're now saying about him on TV is not true."

I winced as he continued to preach. "You people in the United States really don't realize what was happening in Chile in those days," he said. "There were revolutionaries everywhere and the economy was in the tank."

Then he added, "Have you noticed that Chile has changed in the last 40 years? We're not a third world country anymore. You can thank Pinochet for that."

Pinochet inherited the "Chicago Boys," a team of technocrats who, months before the coup, put through a radical plan to overhaul the country's battered economy. Several had studied with Nobel Prize winner Milton Friedman at the University of Chicago and embraced his notions of free-market forces and monetarism.

The military government implemented widespread economic reforms, including currency stabilization, tariff cutting, opening Chile's markets to global trade, restricting labor unions, privatizing social security, and the privatization of hundreds of state-controlled industries.

But economic transformation in the early 1980s was slow and painful, provoking a deep recession that left more than a third of the work force without jobs. Attempts at strikes and protests were ruthlessly put down by Pinochet's secret police. That repression gave the free-market policies time to take hold.

During the years when Chile's government was regarded with international opprobrium, foreign investment was stunted. But to the delight of the business community, that had changed. Chilean products were welcomed everywhere abroad. The Christian Democrat administration was not inclined to tinker with the roaring economic machine they inherited from the Pinochet administration.

Since the mid-1980s, the country's gross domestic product has grown an average of more than six percent a year, the most impressive performance in Latin America. The new policies produced what came to be known as the "Miracle of Chile."

Those policies also dramatically increased economic inequality. The rich got richer. The poor didn't.

I first met Col. Pinochet in 1963 at a social function at the U.S. Consulate in Antofagasta. He had been assigned as commander of the "Esmeralda" regiment of the 1st Army Division four years earlier.

He was cordial, but stiff, and was always in his formal, ceremonial uniform when he was out in public. The Antofagasta newspaper, "*El*

Mercurio," treated him as a celebrity, with photos on page one, but he rarely made news. The military commander was seen as an integral part of the community, often appearing at social, political and religious functions alongside the Catholic bishop, Francisco de Borja Valenzuela Rios.

He was a native of Valparaiso, the son of French settlers who had come to Chile more than a century before. He was taught in Catholic primary and secondary schools and then entered the Military School in Santiago. He graduated in 1937 and rapidly went through the ranks. In 1968 he was promoted to brigadier general and commander in chief of the 6th Division in Iquique, a port north of Antofagasta.

Pinochet never saw any action in combat during his entire career. Chile's last military engagements were in the 19th century. The War of the Pacific in 1879-83 bolstered Chile's borders in the north at the expense of Bolivia and Peru. There was a short civil war and regime change in 1891.

Pinochet, who was in charge of a detention camp for Chilean communists in 1948, first met Salvador Allende, a young Chilean senator, who was visiting the camp. Two decades later, at age 55 and already a general, he was appointed post commander of the Santiago army garrison.

Soon after taking office, President Allende was facing stiff public opposition for many of his Socialist economic policies. A general strike paralyzed Santiago in the late 1972 and Allende called upon Pinochet to impose a state of emergency in the capital.

Pinochet enforced a curfew, ordered the arrest of several hundred demonstrators on both the left and the right, announcing, "I will not tolerate agents of chaos no matter what their political ideology."

The president was impressed at Pinochet's apparent neutral stance. Allende felt he could count on the general to uphold the Chilean military's century-old tradition of loyalty to civilian government. In August 1973, Allende appointed Pinochet commander in chief of the army.

Less than three weeks later, Pinochet's armed forces overthrew the government and President Allende was dead.

Resources:

Jonathan Kandell, New York Times, Dec. 11, 2006; "Dictator who ruled by Terror"

Monte Reel and J.Y. Smith, Washington Post, Dec. 11, 2006; "A Chilean Dictator's Dark Legacy"

Jonathan Franklin, The Guardian, Sept. 11, 2014; "U.S. Considered Offering Asylum"

"Augusto Pinochet," Wikipedia, the free encyclopedia, as of April 17, 2015

BBC, Sept. 11, 1973; "President overthrown in Chile coup"

CHAPTER SEVEN

Photo by Peter A. Geniesse

Father Alberto Hurtado, S.J., was canonized in 2004, becoming Chile's second saint after St. Teresa de Jesus, a Discalced Carmelite nun who died at the age of 19 in 1920 and is honored at this shrine in Los Andes, Chile.

"If we were to start a campaign of love for the poor and homeless, we would in a short time do away with the depressing scenes of begging and children sleeping in the doorways.
–Alberto Hurtado

CHAPTER SEVEN

ST. ALBERTO HURTADO

1901-1952
Santiago, Chile   2004

> *"Está muy bién no hacer el mal*
> It's very good not to do bad
> *Pero está muy mal no hacer el bién."*
> But it's very bad not to do good.

It's the anthem of a modern day saint, a 20th century do-gooder. It's the story of a Catholic priest who didn't dodge the tough issues facing both the church and society in modern Chile.

He wasn't a martyr. He died in 1952 of pancreatic cancer at the age of 51. He wasn't known as a miracle worker, although he was credited with at least two miracles. He didn't have the stigmata, or the traditional glow of holiness. He didn't found a religious order. Nor was he a theologian.

He wasn't anything like Chile's only other saint, St. Teresa de los Andes, a sickly child who died in her teens a century ago and was reported to have special powers.

Alberto Hurtado Cruchaga was called a communist. But he was canonized a saint in 2005.

He was a labor leader in the trenches, a crusader for social justice, a church critic and an advocate for laymen, and above all a friend to the poor.

I never met the man. But I knew him by way of the legacy of his works and through friendship with his many disciples. Father Ignacio Vergara, S.J., a worker priest in the slums of Antofagasta, was a colleague of Padre Alberto and a friend of mine. Father Renato Poblete, S.J., served as chaplain of *Hogar de Cristo,* housing projects for the homeless throughout Chile, including *El Nortero* branch in Antofagasta.

Padre Alberto was best known throughout Latin America for his *Hogar de Cristo* initiative. It's now a Chilean public institution of charity that serves 25,000 people in extreme poverty each month at more than 500 venues in the country.

In April 1987, Pope John Paul II, who declared Padre Alberto "blessed" in 1994, visited the *Hogar de Cristo* in Santiago during his six-day pilgrimage to Chile. I recall being energized at learning of the beatification of an "old friend." But I thought that would be the religious end of the line for his public salvation. There were some, mostly on the political right, who didn't think he was all that holy.

My wife and I were in Chile on vacation, my first revisit in 40 years. Imagine my shock and amazement as we strolled through Santiago's central square which fronts *La Moneda,* the presidential palace, on a Sunday morning in spring. The picnic tables were filled with old men playing chess, and newspaper vendors were hawking the latest news.

Huge page one headlines said it all that day, Oct. 23, 2005. "*Padre Alberto Es Santo.*"

A large contingent of Chileans, including President Ricardo Lagos, and a number of high-ranking Chilean politicians who once were students of Padre Alberto, were on hand in Rome to witness the canonization of Chile's "favorite son" by Pope Benedict XVI.

The crowd in St. Peter's Square, including an estimated 8,000 Chileans, cheered as the pope canonized the country's second saint. The Jesuit priest who smiled down at them from a tapestry on the basilica's façade, was "truly a contemplative in action," the pope said.

Hurtado was hailed as a social reformer, theologian, journalist, inspired preacher, union activist, youth leader, educator and revered public figure.

"He lived in an act of love of God, which translated constantly into one or another act of love for his neighbor," a colleague said.

He learned compassion from his mother. "It is good to put your hands together in prayer," she said. "But it is better to open them in order to give."

Padre Alberto did both. "Every poor person, every vagrant, every beggar is Christ himself who is carrying his cross," he said. "As such we ought to love him and care for him.

"We are directly responsible for the existence of beggars and anti-social behavior," he said. "We pay them salaries of misery, we close the doors to their education, we keep them in promiscuity, sleeping in human heaps, like bundles, scarcely covering themselves with indecent rags."

Hurtado's views did not receive a universal welcome. In circles of church hierarchy – even among his brother Jesuits – he was denounced as a radical. "Just what we needed," one of his detractors said. "The communist virus inside the Catholic Church!"

Alberto was born in Viña del Mar in January 1901. Four years later he was an orphan, when his father died and his mother had to sell their belongings to pay the family's debts. He and his brother went to live with relatives and were often moved from one family to another. At an early age, he felt empathy for the poor, joining the Sodality of Our Lady and spending most Sunday afternoons in poor neighborhoods.

He entered the Jesuit novitiate in Chillán in 1923 and then was sent to Spain to study philosophy and theology. In 1931 he continued his studies at Louvain in Belgium, where he was ordained a priest and obtained a doctorate in pedagogy and psychology. When he returned to Chile in 1936, he taught at *La Universidad Católica* in Santiago.

In 1940, he was appointed archdiocesan director of the Catholic Action youth movement and the following year he was named national director of the group. Many credit that organization with sustaining the Church's continued existence in Chile well into the 1960s.

In 1944, while giving a retreat, Padre Alberto appealed to his audience to consider the plight of poor people, especially the number of homeless children roaming the streets of Santiago. The retreatants responded, and so did Padre Alberto who opened home-like housing for the children. He took in all children in need of food and shelter, abandoned or not.

He purchased a green pickup truck and monitored the streets at night, offering lodging and meals for one night or more. It was estimated that between 1945 and 1951 more than 850,000 children received some help from the program.

In 1945, he visited the United States to study "Boys Town" to consider how it could be adapted to his country. The last six years of his life were dedicated to the development of new ways for "*El Hogar*" to assist the needy.

He built facilities for women and for men. The shelters multiplied and were designed to meet the needs of all, offering such things as rehabilitation centers and trade schools, and included serving terminally ill patients, destitute elders and young people with substance abuse problems.

He often was at odds with the Catholic hierarchy by his writings and his programs for the poor. There was much social inequality in Chile during this period, and conservative Catholics had difficulty accepting the Vatican's social justice teachings.

As late as 1931, the Santiago archdiocese refused to publish *Quadragesimo Anno,* the papal encyclical on workers' rights. When a group of clergy urged reconsideration, Archbishop José Horacio Campillo declined. "It's necessary to protect Catholics from the imprudent acts of the pope," he said.

Padre Alberto chastised his fellow Catholics for not meeting the needs of the poor. "We Catholics are like cattle, asleep, untroubled by any social ties with our fellow human beings," he wrote. His book, entitled "Is Chile a Catholic Country?" also drew fire from his superiors. A 1939 survey of Chilean religious practices found that only 9 percent of women and 3.5 percent of men regularly attended Mass. Conservative Catholics took issue with his findings, some labeling him a communist.

In 1947, Padre Alberto, inspired by the social teachings of the church, entered the labor movement. He founded the Chilean Trade Union Association to train leaders and instill Christian values in Chile's unions. He wrote three books on the subject: "Social Humanism," "The Christian Social Order," and "Trade Unions," which he wrote two years before he died.

He served as confessor to the Falange Nacional, the precursor to the Christian Democratic Party, the banner of several presidents and a force in Chilean politics.

"If we were to start a campaign of love for the poor and homeless, we would in a short time do away with depressing scenes of begging, children sleeping in doorways and women with babies in their arms fainting in our streets," he wrote.

Padre Alberto was diagnosed with pancreatic cancer in 1952, just 15 years into his mission to change Chilean society. Day after day, the media kept the country informed of his state of health. By the time of his death on Aug. 18, 1952, he had become a national hero.

True to the faith he had been professing all his life, he gracefully accepted his fate. On his deathbed he was asked how he felt about his life fulfilled. He praised the Lord and said, *"Muy contento, Señor. Muy contento."*

Resources:

"Home of Christ," by Wikipedia, the free encyclopedia, as of April 4, 2015

Alberto Hurtado, by Thinkjesuit.org, as of April 19, 2015

Alberto Hurtado, by Wikipedia, the free encyclopedia, as of April 18, 2015

Alberto Hurtado Cruchaga, by Vatican News Service, as of April 19, 2015

Luis E. Quezada, The Word Among Us; "I'm Content, Lord," August 2006.

V.R. Alvarez, Nacional de Santiago; "Vaticano Reconoce Milagro," 3 de Abril de 2004.

Chapter Eight

Photo by Peter A. Geniesse

The 1963 missionary team in Antofagasta, Chile, included, from left, volunteer teacher Peter A. Geniesse, school principal Father George Protopapas, O.M.I., volunteer nurse Genevieve Zandala, PAVLA director Father Ray Zagorski and Chilean worker priest Father Ignacio Vergara, S.J.

CHAPTER EIGHT

'APOSTOLIC TOURISTS'

Antofagasta, Chile   1963-67

Some called us "Apostolic Tourists."

They said we weren't real missionaries. Just short-timers on a Christian adventure in South America.

But we were members of the Papal Volunteers for Latin America, the grand experiment in lay Catholicism that grew out of the Second Vatican Council. We didn't last long. PAVLA floundered and faded from the scene in less than a decade.

We were part of the call by Pope John XXIII for religious orders and Catholic dioceses to send 10 percent of their priests and nuns to help bolster the faith in Latin America. That was a dream largely unfulfilled.

It was anticipated that as many as 20,000 priests and religious would take up the call. By 1970, only 1,622 had signed up. PAVLA's lay volunteers numbered about 400 in the field in 1965, and their numbers dropped to 251 just two years later.

Our team from the Green Bay, Wis., Diocese consisted of five volunteers, two nurses and three teachers, one imported from Canada. Jeannine Ducharme, from Alberta, was added to our ranks in Antofagasta when the diocesan volunteer list grew short. Genevieve Zandala, a nurse from Manitowoc, Wis., was the pioneer who served all alone in a small village in central Mexico before being reassigned to Chile. I joined her in the fall of 1963 and within a year we were accompanied by Ducharme and Carol Reinkober, a nurse from Chilton, Wis., and Jim Schaefer, a teacher from Green Bay, Wis.

PAVLA was not a household name in Chile, or anywhere else in Latin America for that matter. We labeled ourselves as members of the "Catholic Peace Corps." People around the globe knew of the Peace Corps. At one time there were 18 Peace Corps volunteers in Antofagasta. And throughout the Third World, their ranks were legion with 220,000 volunteers in 140 countries.

Many of us had little training, prior to "language" school, and virtually no supervision in the field. We had our assignments, requested by the bishop of Antofagasta, but we were essentially free labor, with stipends and expenses paid through our home dioceses. Most of us found time to travel throughout the Third World on the cheap. Jeannine Ducharme rode a boxcar across the continent to attend Carnival in Rio de Janiero. But I outdistanced most of the volunteers.

Early on, I had a lot of time, as my career teaching English to sixth grade boys at Colegio San José was cut short by a disciplinary rule. I chastised a rascal pupil with a casual swat on the butt — not unlike my upbringing — and his wealthy parents called for my scalp. After two months in the classroom, I was fired and on my own. No job, no place to live, 8,000 miles from home and no plane ticket.

Bishop Francisco de Borja Valenzuela Rios had mercy on me. He offered me a part-time job, putting out a weekly newsletter of diocesan notices and happenings, along with analysis from the proceedings at the Second Vatican Council. It was just a two-page bulletin that was posted in the churches throughout the diocese. I subscribed to a couple of Vatican Council news services, and selected mostly liberal views attributed to the Chilean hierarchy for publication.

Chilean bishops, with the exception of Antofagasta's prelate, formed one of the most liberal contingents in Rome, under the direction of Raúl Cardinal Silva of Santiago. It was right up my alley. Many of the Vatican Council's issues had been aired during my training just months before at Ivan Illich's boot camp at Cuernavaca, Mexico.

Needless to say, when Bishop Valenzuela returned from Rome, I was out of another job. But the few *Escudos* I received didn't pay the rent, anyway. I landed a part-time position teaching English to adults at the American Institute, and I applied for a job at the *Universidad del Norte*, a fledging Jesuit university founded just a half-dozen years earlier on the outskirts of Antofagasta.

The university had lofty ambitions, but only a few academic programs and perhaps an enrollment of no more than 500 students. Since I had a journalism degree from the University of Notre Dame and a couple of years' experience in newspaper work in the United States, I was seen as a valuable classroom asset, especially if I didn't need to be paid. I taught a writing class in "Spanglish," and was soon promoted to head of the journalism "department."

The university's vice president, Sohel Riffka, was a go-getter. He had visions of building a major university on the edge of the Atacama Desert. He traveled to the United States to promote his ideas and returned to Antofagasta with volumes and volumes of specifications of surplus commodities being warehoused in the U.S. Everything from heavy building equipment to outfitting classrooms and laboratories were available to Third World countries that could designate and prove a need.

He recruited me to write grant proposals that, if successful, would dramatically change the face of the *Universidad del Norte*. And he promised I'd get a paycheck.

I paged through the manuals to assess the available surplus products and the university's needs, which were many. There were thousands of items, big and small. Riffka said I was to build a case for "everything on the list. If we can't use it," he said, "we can sell it."

When he suggested I put together a package to engage a five-story crane, when the tallest building on the campus was two stories, I refused. I also didn't get a paycheck that week.

All totaled, the grant proposals I eventually submitted easily exceeded $1 million in surplus goods. Much of it was focused on a projected marine biology program, a natural for a university just offshore of the Pacific Ocean.

In 2004, my wife Jill and I visited Antofagasta for the first time in nearly 40 years. *La Universidad del Norte* had grown up. The campus of temporary buildings scattered about the sand dunes serving 500 students or so had become a major university, with an enrollment of 20,000 and multi-story buildings clustered about landscaped quads. And yes, there was a major complex devoted to marine biology, dedicated in the name of a colleague of mine.

I had arrived in Chile on a tourist card, and my time was running out. I was in need of permanent residency papers, available only in Santiago, 700 miles away. Or at a Chilean embassy or consulate in another country. A friend suggested that the most convenient way was to travel to La Paz, Bolivia. Besides there was a once-a-week train leaving from downtown Antofagasta. He didn't mention it was a 52-hour trip, or that Bolivia still didn't have diplomatic relations with Chile.

It all stemmed from the War of the Pacific in the late 1800s when Chile victoriously annexed a large swath of Atacama Desert land, including Antofagasta, effectively blocking Bolivia's access to the Pacific.

And it became another foreign adventure into the unknown for this "apostolic tourist."

The narrow gauge train, a throwback to the days before the war when it served nitrate mining stations throughout the *altiplano*, at one time was the highest railroad in the world, reaching altitudes above 13,000 feet.

The train chugged through the *cordillera de la costa* and entered the barren desert where temperatures reached 100 degrees by noon and 30 degrees by sundown. The grade up to the Andes was so foreboding that the train inched its way at times, and passengers got off the train for a slow stroll. It was the lifeblood for the tiny settlements along the way which sold hot tea in Coke bottles at night and freshly slaughtered llamas during the day.

Two days and two nights later, the train pulled into La Paz. Slogans on billboards saying *"Nuestro Derecho, El Mar"* hinted at what was to come. Landlocked Bolivia still hadn't gotten over losing its right to the sea.

The sign in the window of the tiny Chilean consulate said "closed for the holidays." That meant at least a two-week delay. Perhaps, a passerby said, Chile's consulate in Oruru might be open. So I got on a 3rd class bus and arrived in the tin mining capital right in the midst of a bloody labor strike. A Canadian Oblate priest rescued me from the street battles and escorted me to his house, guarded day and night by indigenous workers. And, no, he said, there's never been a Chilean consulate in Oruru. "They don't like Chileans here," he said.

Maybe there's a consulate in Cochabama, he said.

It was New Year's Day when a tiny bus, loaded with revelers, went down the mountain at record speed. The driver had made a bet with a friend in Oruru, altitude 11,800 feet, that he could make it to Cochabama, elevation 8,400 feet, in less than an hour. It was a one-lane gravel road, carved into the side of a steep mountain, with both a fantastic and terrifying vista. The driver made it; his passengers, after a night of partying, didn't fare so well physically.

No, there was no consulate in Cochabama. So it was back to La Paz, on a different bus on a different route. A group of Papal Volunteers from St. Louis, Mo., classmates of mine at Cuernavaca, put me up for the duration.

Ten days later, I boarded the train to Antofagasta, with a Chilean permanent residency card in hand. This time it was mostly downhill, and took only 44 hours.

It wasn't long before I was off to Santiago to meet with other Papal Volunteers, several of whom worked, for free, at *La Universidad Católica*. Every six months or so, we would schedule a meeting or a retreat, often in the capitals of Santiago or Lima, Peru. We traveled by 3rd class buses and creaky trains and sometimes in the back of trucks. We free-loaded at the homes of other volunteers, or at priest rectories or school sites. We often ate off the street and on the road.

Which brings me to the *altiplano* of Peru, the home of Cuzco and Machu Picchu and *anticuchos,* those llama hearts grilled on a brazier and served on a skewer. Following a Papal Volunteer retreat in Lima, I accepted an invitation to visit colleagues in Arequipa, Puno, Sicuani and other indigenous communities on the 12,000-foot plain.

It's another world up there in llama-land. If only I had been prepared for it. Before I had left Antofagasta on a 30-hour bus trip, I could have had a gamma globulin injection. A Peace Corps staffer was making the rounds in Antofagasta, checking on the health of the volunteers and updating their shots. He felt sorry for me, not having medical care, and offered to give me a "gamma" to boost my immunity against diseases I'd likely face in primitive Peru.

But I foolishly said no. I would have to sit on bench seats on a bus for unending hours, and that shot in the butt just wouldn't make my life more comfortable.

So, I got hepatitis. My eyes turned yellow and my urine turned orange and I felt miserable all over. Back in Antofagasta, I moved into a rooming house to wait out the symptoms. I was supposed to be bedridden, but after a month of boredom, I went back on the job at the university, and I suffered a relapse.

This time a physician ordered me hospitalized.

Antofagasta had a beautiful soccer stadium, with luxuriant green grass contrasting the desert sands. I could see it from my room in the dilapidated hospital on the hill that lacked for paint and basic services. Most of the patients were lined up on cots, at least 12 to a ward.

I got the hospital's lone single room. I was told it was reserved for dignitaries. The giant bed measured eight-feet long and was three feet off the floor. It was fabricated in the hospital shop to accommodate a request by the French government. French Premier Charles De Gaulle had planned a goodwill tour of Latin America, and in case of an emergency, he'd need a comfortable hospital bed.

So I was atop the dignitary bed when the nurse came in the room to spray DDT to fend off the termites that were chewing the ceiling's wooden panels. She advised me to put the sheet over my head. When the mist settled, she then proceeded to poke me with a needle to draw a blood sample.

Friends said it was probably then when I started to get delirious. I was reading Time Magazine when I noticed that King Baudouin of

Belgium had cancelled his upcoming visit to Chile as he had come down with infectious hepatitis. I wrote him a sympathetic letter, saying I, too, had Belgian blood and wondering if we Belgians were especially susceptible to the disease.

Several weeks later, a nurse came into the room and handed me a letter. It bore the stamp of King Baudouin. He wrote that he appreciated my sentiments, and that he'd like to get together with me when he comes to Antofagasta in a few months to honor Father Gustavo Le Paige. He was the famed Belgian Jesuit anthropologist who studied the *Atacameños,* the first inhabitants of San Pedro de Atacama, and created a museum in their name.

Thus started the legend of the crazy American who cavorted with kings and French premiers. To further embellish my reputation, I wrote a note to a star female writer for a Santiago magazine citing the ten reasons why I wouldn't marry her. She didn't respond.

I was not without guests in that hospital room. The nurses catered to my needs, shopping the open market daily for fresh fruit and playing board games with their friends aboard the giant bed when they were off duty. I was having a good time, at age 27 and single. However, my doctor said I wasn't getting better and suggested I return to the United States. Father Ray Zagorski, the PAVLA director concurred, and sent me a check for a flight back home.

It was mid-September 1965 when I boarded a Pan American plane after a big sendoff at the Antofagasta airport. The "Apostolic Tourist" was on his way home to get a job, get married and live a normal life. I had an offer from the Maryknoll Fathers to head a Catholic news service agency in Lima. It was tempting, but I also had a girlfriend back home in Green Bay, Wis., who already had waited too long for me to grow up.

So I got well in the U.S., landed a job as a reporter for The Post-Crescent in Appleton, Wis., married Jill Seroogy, and day-dreamed my way through Latin America for the next 30 years.

Chapter Nine

Photo by Peter A. Geniesse
Pat Pyeatt, an Oklahoma man for all seasons, served several terms as a PAVLA lay missioner in Guatemala before becoming both a Sikh named Pritam Singh and a skilled chiropractor in northern California.

> *"He was not of this world. He was always in the heavens.*
> *He just came to pay his karma."*
> *—Of Pritam Singh*

CHAPTER NINE

'SIKH' PAT PYEATT

1938-2002
Santiago Atitlán, Guatemala   1971

He was a good one, this Papal Volunteer, engineer and mystic who left a lasting legacy in the Tzutuhil Indian village on the banks of Lago Atitlán and just about everywhere he sojourned.

He was my friend and mentor at Ivan Illich's CIDOC training center in Cuernavaca, Mexico. We traveled on 3rd class buses throughout Mexico and we kept in touch when I went to Chile and he set off for Guatemala. When my tour of duty was up, he visited me in Green Bay, Wis., on New Year's Eve where we witnessed the 1967 Packers-Cowboys "Ice Bowl" together in minus-48 degree wind-chill temperatures.

He insisted that I make a return visit to his idyllic haven in Guatemala where there's no ice. So in the winter of 1971, my wife Jill, our two-year-old son Peter and I set out in our station wagon for Panajachel, Guatemala.

There was a civil war going on ever since 1960, and the indigenous population was the principal target of the state-sponsored militia, but we were told the village of Santiago was a safe place and the government was promoting tourism around one of the most beautiful lakes in the world.

There were no decent roads linking the lakeside villages, so we boarded the aging mail boat from Panajachel for the 40-minute trip to Santiago. Lago Atitlán is the deepest lake in Central America, reaching a depth of more than 1,100 feet. It's of volcanic origin and there are three still active volcanos, two that embrace Santiago at 10,000 feet.

The volcanos were sending their vapors into the blue sky as we reached Santiago. It was market day and the village square was bustling with tourists and Mayan descendants in native costume. We visited the Catholic church, inquiring about the whereabouts of Pat Pyeatt. We were told he had suddenly returned to Oklahoma, as his life had been threatened by the militia for defending the Tzutuhil people.

Pyeatt was one of the pioneers of the mission sent by the Diocese of Oklahoma City and Tulsa to serve indigenous Catholics. In late 1963 he joined Father Ramon Carlin, the pastor of the team of priests, nuns and laypeople, who allied themselves with the oppressed poor, Tzutuhil Indians and the mixed blooded Ladinos. It was an unusual assignment for them as the Catholic Church itself in Oklahoma was considered "mission" territory until 1905.

They developed a comprehensive plan to serve "the most destitute people on earth." The missionaries divided their work into four areas: worship, catechetics, health and agriculture. The Tzutuhil language was put down in writing for the first time. Native trained catechists created a radio school. A health clinic evolved into a hospital. And model farming was at the heart of agriculture.

Pyeatt had an exceptional aptitude for learning languages. He was fluent in Spanish after a couple of months of classes in Mexico. It didn't take him long to converse in the Tzutuhil language, either. He was in charge of setting up agricultural and small industrial cooperatives and credit unions. He taught the farmers modern techniques of soil preparation. He also made friends of the people who were considered adversaries of the government.

When Father Carlin left to work in the new linguistic institute in Antigua, Guatemala, he was succeeded in Santiago by Father Stanley Rother of Okarche, OK. Rother finished the translation of the New Testament into Tzutuhil and he won the hearts of the natives, but not those of the oligarchy and its militia.

The times were tense in Santiago. Indigenous people were assumed to be supporters of the guerrillas who were fighting against the government, and they were targeted for brutal reprisals. At least 300 Maya from Santiago are believed to have disappeared during the Guatemalan Civil War which lasted 36 years.

There were numerous atrocities in the hills of Santiago, but one in particular made news. On Dec. 2, 1990, a spontaneous protest march to the army base on the edge of the village was met by gunfire by the Guatemalan Army and the massacre of 14 unarmed civilians, and the wounding of 21 others. International pressure forced the Guatemalan government to close the base and declare Santiago Atitlán a "military-free zone."

It is estimated that throughout the country 200,000 civilians were killed or "disappeared" between 1960 and 1996, most at the hands of the military, the police or intelligence services. The government forces have been condemned for "death squads" and for "scorched earth" policies and officials have been tried and convicted of genocide.

The political situation in Santiago became volatile during Father Rother's early years, and twice he was sent back to Oklahoma after receiving death threats. But he didn't stay long in his home town. "The shepherd cannot run," he told his family. "My people need me."

On July 28, 1981, shortly after he returned to Santiago, Father Rother was murdered in his rectory by a right-wing death squad.

For three years after his assassination, there was no priest at the helm of Oklahoma's mission to the Maya. It was May of 1984 when two Oklahoma bishops, priests and 20 laypeople, including Father Rother's parents, made a pilgrimage to the church of Santiago Atitlán. Among the priests on that mission trip was Father Thomas McSherry, a Tulsa native and priest for the Archdiocese of Oklahoma City.

It was Father McSherry who would build a memorial to Father Rother and to the victims of the Civil War that raged for more than three decades. He served 17 years at Santiago Atitlán, the longest of any cleric, and he built churches as well as homes for the widows of the war. He married and baptized thousands until the Oklahoma Mission was ended in 2001 and the reins were turned over to the local diocese, which now had priests to staff it.

His assessment of the 37 years that Oklahoma priests, nuns and laity served God and the Tzutuhil Indians was simple.

"Missionaries, I think, are like good teachers or mentors," he said. "They give their best and move on."

It was late afternoon when we went down to the docks to board the mail boat for its daily return trip to Panajachel. The wind was picking up, sending ripples, then white caps roiling across the lake. Earlier on the way to Santiago, there were only a dozen tourists on the boat. Now the carrier counted a dozen Tzutuhil Indians as well and one ton of ripe bananas, all on their way to market on the mainland.

The boat sat low in the water and the passengers stood at the rails as the bananas claimed precedence to the bench seats. The boat was overloaded, a scary but not an unusual occurrence in the Third World.

We were but 50 feet from the dock when the motor cut out. The operator fiddled with the engine, and it started. The engine started and stopped a half-dozen times before we were a mile out. The bilge pump then failed, and water sloshed about the deck.

The captain said the boat was carrying too much weight. The tourists said dump the bananas. An Indian said if you want to throw the bananas overboard, you'll have to throw me in first.

The water was rising on the deck, ankle deep. My wife found a lone life preserver under a seat and wrapped our two-year-old son in its straps. The waves and slight movements on deck heightened the danger. The tourists turned to me to negotiate the ton of bananas since I could speak Spanish. But most of the Indians spoke Tzutuhil. Their leader insisted that the bananas were their life and refused to consider dumping them.

The tourists went silent as they pondered their fate. There were no rescue boats on the lake, and only a few fishermen in fragile skiffs were scattered along the shoreline. If the weight shifted and the boat overturned and sunk like a stone in the middle of the lake, we'd all drown. We just couldn't understand why the Indians were willing to die for their produce.

Some of the tourists started to pray, others shared end thoughts as they viewed smoke curling in the sky from two volcanos. One said our story would garner only a paragraph in the *New York Times*. Another reveled in the beauty of the setting sun. Another ignored the crisis with a silly song. It was indeed a ship of fools.

For more than two hours, the engine growled and sputtered and kept hopes alive, only to bob in the waves in silence. But Panajachel did draw closer with each spurt of power. As the captain steered the boat onto the wharf, the Tzutuhil leader turned to me and said in Spanish, "I told you we would make it."

Pat Pyeatt couldn't stay away for long. He learned to love the Tzutuhil people, and when his three-year PAVLA commitment was up, he signed up for another three years. Then he left Santiago Atitlán to try to figure out what he was going to do with the rest of his life.

He was born in Tulsa and received a master's degree in engineering from Oklahoma State University in 1963. But he still wasn't sure he wanted to be an engineer. He preferred poetry and languages and theology – and travel. So when his diocese was looking for a lay volunteer for their mission team in Santiago Atitlan, he jumped at the chance.

In December of 1969, he headed south to Chile, enrolled at La Universidad Católica in Santiago and studied theology, anthropology and linguistics in graduate school. Then he decided to become a Catholic priest, was accepted in the seminary, and suddenly had second thoughts.

He studied yoga in 1972, and was intrigued by the teachings of Yogi Bhajam, who was known to his followers as Siri Singh Sahib, a spiritual cult leader who introduced Kundalini Yoga to the U.S. Bhajam exerted influence over 300 centers in 35 countries.

Ever in search of the meaning of life, he decided to adopt the Sikh way, and changed his name to Pritam Singh.

Pritam Singh returned to the United States, made his way to Wisconsin and gave me a call. He said we had a lot of catching up to do. He had gotten married and had a son. I invited them for dinner, and put together a fantastic meal of langostinos, ribeye steaks, Chilean wine and all the fixings we both had enjoyed in Chile.

He said he was Sikh. And I thought he said he was sick.

Two hours later, they drove up the driveway at my house in Neenah, Wis. Pat Pyeatt got out of the car putting his bare feet in the snow. He was wearing a white turban, had a long red beard and wore a white sheath that reached to his ankles. His wife, introduced as Siri Pritam Kaur, also was barefoot and was nursing a child.

He said his name now was Pritam Singh, and that he was a Sikh, and thus a vegetarian, and he couldn't drink wine or eat meat or langostinos. So we served a big bowl of salad greens, and talked about olden days and his new life.

Pritam Singh said he believed in natural healing, and his new life was one as a chiropractor in Yuba City, California. Later he received a doctorate from Life Chiropractic College –West and spent years learning and teaching advanced chiropractic techniques.

He also was an accomplished poet, "learned in the ways of the heart," according to friends. "He was an uncompromising lover of truth and a scholar."

He was married for 27 years to Siri Pritam Kaur. They had a daughter and two sons.

Pritam Singh died of cancer on April 26, 2002. His poetic signature read:

"He was not of this world. He was always in the heavens. He just came to pay his karma."

CHAPTER TEN

Photo by Peter A. Geniesse

Gail Phares, a former Maryknoll missionary in Central America, formed Witness for Peace and her efforts helped end the Contra War in Nicaragua.

"Witness for Peace volunteers had the longest non-violent presence in an active war zone of anyone in history."
–Gail Phares

CHAPTER TEN

'WITNESS' GAIL PHARES

1940 –
Managua, Nicaragua   1983

She witnessed the atrocities, the killings, the abject poverty, the hopelessness of millions of Latin Americans, all victims of U.S. policies unraveled.

If that was ever to change, she knew she would need many more witnesses from the United States to tell their story back home.

That was three decades and thousands of witnesses ago.

Gail Phares, 75, a former Maryknoll missioner to Central America, is still recruiting volunteers and challenging them "to do hard things." She is still forming "beloved communities" from like-minded strangers. She is still leading Witness for Peace delegations into war zones and returning them to the U.S. to demonstrate and lobby for change.

It all started back in the spring of 1983. Phares had seen too much violence during her missionary days in Nicaragua and Guatemala. When she returned to her home community, she became determined to do something about it. She formed an interfaith task force in Raleigh, N.C., and convinced others to travel to Nicaragua on a fact-finding mission to learn first-hand of the fallout from the U.S.-funded Contra War.

The group visited El Porvenir on the Honduran border in the wake of a Contra mortar attack that had destroyed numerous peasant huts.

"We went to one shack where the mother was still standing in shock," Phares recalled. "The tiny house had been hit by mortars and her daughter had just been taken by ambulance to Jalapa."

But while the group was there, no shells fell. They could see the Contra encampment across the river, but their guns remained silent.

"If all it takes to stop the killing is to have Americans here, let's call for a vigil," Phares' colleague said.

Nicaraguan government officials reluctantly endorsed the idea. The group returned to the U.S., determined to hold a large peace vigil in the embattled frontier town of Jalapa. They recruited 153 volunteers from 37 states and on July 4, 1983, the Americans stood hand-in-hand with Nicaraguan peasants, and eye-to-eye with the Contras across the border.

"We formed a big circle and held hands with mothers who had lost children to the Contra attacks," Phares said. There were no violent incidents that day.

The Carolina Interfaith Task Force on Central America had just given birth to "Witness for Peace." That October a founding retreat in Philadelphia set the agenda.

"We defined ourselves as a non-violent, faith-based movement that opposed the United States' covert and overt intervention in Nicaragua," Phares said. "Our purpose was to change U.S. foreign policy."

Each month, several smaller delegations were sent into the war zones. By June 1984, some 200 people from all 50 states had traveled to Nicaragua. Witness for Peace had become a nationwide movement in less than one year, raising more than $1 million.

"We trained people in nonviolence and we created beloved communities," she said. Over a five-year period, WFP had as many as 40 long-term volunteers, two-by-two, in Contra combat areas in Nicaragua.

"We had the longest nonviolent presence in an active war zone of anyone in history," Phares said. "I remember going into villages and there were mortar shells right over our heads. Our young volunteers saw people and houses blown up. Several suffered post-traumatic stress," she added.

One delegation from New York was held by the Contras at Rio San Juan, and two other long-term volunteers also were later kidnapped.

While President Ronald Reagan was equating the Contras with America's Founding Fathers, Phares said that some members of Congress and the media were beginning to turn away and pay attention to the testimony of Witness for Peace leaders.

"We had a lot to do with the Boland Amendment," Phares said. "They couldn't give money to the Contras. And the Marines couldn't invade because of our presence."

The measure limited U.S. government assistance to the Contras for the purpose of overthrowing the Nicaraguan government. This led to the Iran-Contra affair which illegally circumvented the law. Millions of dollars were generated to support the Contras via secret sales of military missiles to Iran.

The war in Nicaragua was winding down when WFP was asked in 1989 to help ease the return of Guatemalan refugees from camps in southern Mexico. Volunteers accompanied thousands of returning refugees over the course of several years and WFP maintained a presence in Guatemala for more than a decade.

WFP sent several delegations to Haiti in 1992 as international observers to stand by the people in crisis in the wake of President Jean-Bertrand Aristide's ouster. In 1999, WFP began a permanent presence in Cuba to expose the human cost of the punishing U.S. embargo. The following year WFP opened an office in Colombia to document the effects of the United States' multi-billion-dollar military and counter-narcotics package.

Phares led a 25-member fact-finding delegation to Colombia in 2001 and returned two years later with 100 volunteers, including religious and union leaders and congressional staffers.

Witness for Peace has undergone major transformations in recent years. The heart of the movement is still sending volunteers on fact-finding missions. But the issues and the WFP activities vary from country to country. Now it's not war in Nicaragua, but debt. It's not refugees in Mexico, but NAFTA. In Cuba, the U.S. embargo is the issue; in Colombia, the drug-driven counter-insurgency. For all four countries, the thrust is economic.

Phares said WFP had to refocus its efforts after the Contra war. "We worked to end the war in Nicaragua, but we always knew that the underpinning was injustice. So we began to work on economic justice issues."

Staffers now study such things as national debt effects, the World Bank and the International Monetary Fund. Delegations are brought to Washington, D.C., for briefings from IMF. Then they travel to Nicaragua and other Latin American countries to see how those positions play out.

In the mid-1990s, WFP organized vigils to close the U.S. Army School of the Americas and held protests at the World Bank in Washington, D.C. The staff worked with sweatshop workers in Nicaragua's free trade zone, resulting in their first union contract. In 2002, WFP led the effort to organize the National Mobilization on Colombia which brought 10,000 people to Washington.

It's been more than three decades since Phares created Witness for Peace to end the Contra War in Nicaragua. The movement has now grown to count more than 13,000 "witnesses" in the field and another 20,000 on the home front. It also has expanded to several other Latin countries. WFP now has offices in Nicaragua, Mexico and Colombia and it also operates in Venezuela and Bolivia.

After leading more than 40 delegations, Phares still sees WFP as a vehicle for change. "The purpose of our delegations is to transform people, to help them see things differently and empower them to come home and change policies.

"I believe that this country desperately needs signs of hope," she said. "We just have to keep celebrating life, and forming those beloved communities."

In the fall of 2005, Phares was jailed for deliberately trespassing at the former School of the Americas at Fort Benning, Georgia. (The U.S. Army since changed the name of the program to the Western Hemisphere Institute for Security Cooperation.)

She was one of 19,000 protesters who attended a two-day rally aimed at closing the military training station for many Latin American military who have been linked to atrocities and assassinations.

When asked why she risked a prison sentence, she responded: "Because they killed my friend Maura Clarke in El Salvador 25 years ago."

Clarke was murdered on Dec. 2, 1980, along with Jean Donovan and sisters Ita Ford and Dorothy Kazel. The slaying of the four churchwomen galvanized the nation and led to closer scrutiny of U.S. policies in Latin America.

"When they killed those four religious women, people said 'something's wrong if our government is supporting people who are raping and killing nuns,'" Phares said.

Three of the five soldiers implicated in those murders were graduates of the U.S. Army School of the Americas. Scores of Latin American soldiers trained at SOA have been implicated in human rights abuses in their own countries.

"Despite a shocking human rights record, this school continues to operate with U.S. taxpayer money," Phares said. "Closing the SOA would send a strong human rights message to Latin America and the world."

As a Maryknoll nun, Phares served with Clarke in Siuna, Nicaragua, from 1963 to 1966. "I still mourn Maura's passing," she said. "It helps me to understand what the Salvadorans, Nicaraguans and Guatemalans feel who have lost parents, friends and children during those awful, awful U.S.-supported wars in Central America."

I first learned of Gail Phares' witness when I was doing a free-lance article on Witness for Peace on the occasion of its 25th anniversary celebration in Washington, D.C.

I realized I had similar experiences during my newspaper assignment in Nicaragua in 1986. I had gone to the frontier with a Sandinista guide to see firsthand how the farmers were faring during the harvest bombardments. It was eerie to see the enemy lined up across the Rio Coco in Honduras. Scary, too. Our Jeep was trapped by the contour of the land, and a single mortar could have taken us out. But not a shot was fired.

I was part of a delegation of reporters from Wisconsin, sent to make sense of the Contra War which essentially pitted President Ronald Reagan against Wisconsin Governor Anthony Earl. The eight-day media tour was sponsored by the Wisconsin Coordinating Council on Nicaragua.

Wisconsin and Nicaragua became "sister states" via the Partners of the Americas program in 1964, an outgrowth of President Kennedy's Alliance for Progress. A dozen Wisconsin communities developed "sister city" relationships with Nicaraguan cities.

"Wisconsin's commitment to Nicaragua has not changed," Earl said during our media sendoff, "even though our national policy has."

All over the country are projects developed with Wisconsin money. There's Colegio Wisconsin, a large grade school in Managua, built with state money after the 1972 earthquake. The University of Wisconsin sent technical assistance to aid in the recovery. The state also provided more than $2 million worth of drugs and hospital supplies.

"Is Wisconsin helping the enemy?" Earl asked. "My answer is that Wisconsin is helping the people of Nicaragua."

Resources:

Peter A. Geniesse, Sojourner's; "Emissaries of Hope," November-December 2003.

SOA Watch, "What is the School of Assassins?"

Wikipedia, the free encyclopedia, "Boland Amendment"

CHAPTER ELEVEN

Photo by Peter A. Geniesse

A crowd estimated at more than 300,000 attended a political rally for Nicaragua's President Daniel Ortega in February of 1990. The banner reads: "We will win and everything will be better."

"Our experience shows that one can be both a believer and a revolutionary and that no unsalvageable contradiction exists between the two."
–Daniel Ortega

CHAPTER ELEVEN

'EL GALLO' DANIEL ORTEGA

1945-
Managua, Nicaragua   1990

No one could believe it, not the Americans, not the Nicaraguans, not the UNO partisans, not the Sandinistas.

They said there just was no way the Sandinistas could lose the election.

The revolutionary heroes who ousted the dreaded dictator Anastacio Somoza a decade earlier still were the darlings. The United States, which invaded Nicaragua seven times in 40 years, helping create the Sandino legend, still was the villain.

They said that UNO, a mishmash of 14 political ideologies from conservative to communist, formed six months earlier for the sole purpose of ousting the FSLN, didn't have a chance with the likes of Violeta Chamorro at the helm.

The FSLN had a lock on the election on Feb. 25, 1990. The Sandinistas had the incumbency advantage, they managed the media, they plastered the cities and countryside with posters, and they could count on thousands of patronage job votes.

When the two nuns were killed by the Contras, and the United States invaded Panama, the FSLN stock shot up. Almost all the polls had Daniel Ortega and his FSLN team with an insurmountable 13- to 15-point lead.

The Sandinista rally drew 300,000 to the plaza in Managua; the UNO rally estimate was about 100,000.

Election observers from the United Nations, the Organization of American States and former U.S. President Jimmy Carter's special team assured that the elections were free and fair.

So, how did President Daniel Ortega lose Nicaragua's first free and fair election? How did Violeta Chamorro, the widow of a newspaper publisher, end the 10-year reign of the Sandinistas, by a 54 to 41 margin, yet?

In the secrecy of the voting booth, Nicaraguans sent a democratic message to the Sandinistas. They were weary of eight years of war and the grinding poverty only a few knew under Somoza. They were turned off by a decade of FSLN unfulfilled promises. They said enough was enough. They voted for change.

Most didn't vote for UNO. They voted against FSLN. Anything would be better, they said.

They called them "Sandalistas," those hordes of left-leaning Americans who descended on this desperately poor nation to assure that the United States wouldn't steal the FSLN victory.

They also came from all over the continent, and many from Europe, to monitor the campaign and the balloting which Nicaragua staged to get the United States off its back.

The elections had been scheduled for the following November but were pushed up to Feb. 25 with the hope that the renewed democracy would help put an end to the Contra War and the U.S. stranglehold on the nation's economy.

Managua teemed with white faces, youths in Nikes, backpacks and FSLN T-shirts. There were middle-aged people with notebooks and cameras, and even some senior citizens, radicals of another era. They belonged to peace and justice groups, to religious ecumenical councils, to solidarity coalitions. More than 400 election observers were representatives of sister cities, with delegations from the Netherlands, West Germany and throughout the U.S., including a 35-member contingent from Wisconsin.

The "Sandalistas" were studded with stars. Actor Ed Asner headed a British delegation. Daryl Hannah, Martin Sheen and rock star Jackson Brown were there. Reggae musician Jimmy Cliff from Jamaica put on a special concert in the plaza after the Sandinista rally. Brian Willson, the man who lost his legs in a U.S. nuclear train protest, was there to give witness to the cause of peace.

It was front page news throughout much of the world, and journalists and media crews flocked to Managua for press credentials. They came from London, and from Santiago, Chile, and from Sydney, Oslo and Tokyo. There were more than 900 registered media a week before the elections.

President Daniel Ortega and Sergio Ramirez, his vice president, were available just about everywhere. Six days before the election, Ortega put on a party for foreign journalists, and more than 1,000 jammed a Managua restaurant to drink free beer and rum and Cokes and get a chance to press the flesh of the president.

The journalists jostled to get in line to take photos and exchange a few words with Ortega, his wife Rosario, and Ramirez. Some women even got a kiss from *"El Gallo"* and a photo souvenir to record the moment.

I shook Ortega's hand and exchanged a few courtesy phrases. When I got to Ramirez, I had the opportunity for a mini-interview. "We met in Madison, Wis., about four years ago," I said. "Do you recall the occasion?"

Ramirez smiled and said, "How could I forget that. Those were the Hasenfus days."

We spoke for a few moments about how Ramirez had met with then-Gov. Anthony Earl and the family of Eugene Hasenfus, the Marinette, Wis., pilot who was shot down over southern Nicaragua while gun-running for the Contras in the fall of 1986.

Hasenfus received a pardon and was released from prison in time for Christmas that year.

"He may be a son-of-a-bitch, but he's our son-of-a-bitch." So said President Franklin D. Roosevelt about Anastacio Somoza, the feared and hated Nicaraguan dictator.

For more than four decades, the Somoza family ruled Nicaragua with an iron fist – and with an open hand. The National Guard, formed and trained by the U.S., was the Somoza family force. There are documented cases of peasant massacres and terrorism where guardsmen confiscated farmland and turned it over to the Somozas

The wealth of the ruling family, accumulated over 40 years in corporate bribes, industrial monopolies, land grabbing and foreign aid siphoning, was enormous.

When Anastacio Somoza fled the country on July 19, 1979, he left behind family holdings worth well over a half-billion dollars. He had already stockpiled at least that much wealth outside of the country. The Somoza family owned 20 per cent of the country's arable land. It also owned 154 of the largest commercial and industrial establishments in the country.

The Somoza family was put in power and kept in power by the United States.

The downfall of the family dynasty started with the 1972 earthquake which killed 10,000, left 250,000 homeless and destroyed much of Managua. The U.S. sent $78 million in aid. The Somoza family took it. There is no evidence of reconstruction in the heart of Managua.

At the end of his reign, Somoza turned to terror, ordering his guardsmen to slaughter peasants and urban dissidents. On three occasions, his air force bombed and strafed Esteli, a city of 50,000, about 100 miles north of Managua.

When Somoza was gunned down on a street corner in Asuncion, Paraguay, reportedly by the Sandinistas, Nicaraguans reveled that he had been "shot like a dog."

The loathing that Nicaraguans display for Somoza is filtered when it comes to his historic benefactor, the United States. There's a strong anti-American sentiment in the country which saw three decades of U.S. Marine occupation.

In 1912, the U.S. sent in its Marines to quell a political rebellion. They didn't leave until 1925, returning the following year and staying until 1933. One year later, Augusto Cesar Sandino (from which comes Sandinistas), who fought against foreign occupation, was assassinated by Somoza forces as he was about to sign a truce in Managua.

"Every one of our national heroes fought against the gringos," one leader said.

Daniel Ortega's mother was imprisoned by Somoza's National Guard on a conspiracy charge when Daniel was growing up. When he was 15 he was arrested for political activities, and he soon joined the Sandinista National Liberation Front (FSLN).

He had a checkered past as a youth and served time for robbing a bank in 1967. He was released in late 1974 along with other Sandinista prisoners in exchange for Somocista hostages. While in prison, Ortega was severely tortured, and upon release, he went to Cuba where he received several months of guerrilla training. He then returned to Nicaragua.

When Somoza was overthrown by the FSLN in July 1979, Ortega became a member of the five-person Junta of National Reconstruction. The other members were Sandinista militant Moises Hassan, novelist Sergio Ramirez, businessman Alfonso Robelo, and Violeta de Barrios Chamorro, the widow of a newspaper editor who was murdered by the Somoza regime.

As the FSLN came to dominate the junta, Robelo and Chamarro resigned, leaving Ortega as the effective leader of the country. The FSLN then embarked on an ambitious program of social reform. It redistributed five million acres of land to 100,000 families, launched a literacy campaign and instituted health programs which rid the country of polio.

The Sandinista government implemented a policy of forced conscription for all men from age 17 to 35. Ortega took a hard line against opposition to his policies. The army massacred 110 miners for demanding payment of back wages. It also killed Miskito Indians and displaced 10,000 indigenous tribesmen in what was referred to as the "politics of ethnocide."

In 1981, U.S. President Ronald Reagan accused the FSLN of joining with Soviet-backed Cuba in supporting Marxist revolutionary movements in other Latin American countries, notably El Salvador. The Reagan administration authorized the Central Intelligence Agency to begin financing, arming and training rebels, some of whom were former officers in Somoza's National Guard.

On March 4, 1983, Pope John Paul II visited Nicaragua, attacked its "People's Church" and had harsh remarks for the five Catholic priests who served in the Sandinista government. American missionaries were split over their allegiance, with those subscribing to "liberation theology" favoring the Sandinistas.

Those included the Rev. Ernesto Cardenal, the minister of culture, and the Rev. Miguel d'Escoto, Nicaragua's foreign minister.

The pope encountered vocal opposition when he spoke at an open air Mass, attended by nearly a half-million people. He said the five priests were breaking church unity by "acting outside or against the will of the bishops." He gave support to the archbishop of Managua, Miguel Obando y Bravo, a vocal critic of the Sandinistas and of the Catholic leaders who sided with them.

In his speech welcoming the pope, Ortega accused the U.S. of "aggressive actions" against Nicaragua and warned that "the footsteps of interventionist boots echo threateningly in the White House and the Pentagon."

Ortega was anxious to demonstrate that Catholicism forms part of the revolution in his remarks at the airport. "Our experience shows that one can be both a believer and a revolutionary and that no unsalvageable contradiction exists between the two," he said.

On Jan. 4, 1982, President Reagan signed the top secret National Security Decision Directive 17, giving the CIA authority to recruit and support the Contras with $19 million in military aid. In 1984, the U.S. Congress approved $24 million in Contra aid.

However, when it was disclosed that the CIA had mined Nicaraguan ports, popular and congressional support waned. Congress cut off all funds for the Contras in 1985 with the third Boland Amendment.

Nevertheless, Reagan continued his campaign to counter Soviet influence in Nicaragua. On May 1, 1985 he declared a "national emergency" and a trade embargo to "deal with the threat."

With Congress blocking further Contra aid, the Reagan administration sought funding from third countries and private sources. Between 1984 and 1986, more than $36 million was raised by the National Security Council with Lt. Col. Oliver North in charge of "The Enterprise."

The secret Enterprise led to the Iran-Contra affair of 1986-87 which facilitated Contra funding through the proceeds of arm sales to Iran.

After the cutoff of U.S. military support, and with both sides facing international pressure to bring an end to the conflict, the Contras agreed to negotiations with the FSLN. With the help of five Central American presidents, including Ortega, it was agreed that a voluntary demobilization of the Contras would start in December 1989 to prepare for the elections in 1990.

The 10-year Contra War was over, with a dead toll of more than 30,000, with the surprising election of the U.S.-backed Violeta Chamorro as president.

In Ortega's concession speech he vowed to keep "ruling from below," a reference to the power the FSLN still wielded in various sectors. He ran for president in 1996, and again in 2001, but lost on both occasions to Arnoldo Alemán and Enrique Bolaños, respectively.

Ortega gave it another try in 2006 and won with 38 per cent of the vote, defeating the mayor of Managua, Herty Lewites, who died several months before the election. The FSLN also won 38 seats in the congressional elections, becoming the largest party in Congress.

Through the years, Ortega's policies became more moderate, and he gradually changed much of his former Marxist stance in favor of democratic socialism. His Roman Catholic faith also became more public, leading Ortega to embrace a variety of socially conservative policies. In 2006, the FSLN endorsed a strict law banning all abortions in Nicaragua.

In 2011, after the Supreme Court cleared the way for his third term as president, Ortega won with 62 per cent of the vote in a five-candidate race.

Resources:

Peter A. Geniesse, The Post-Crescent, Appleton, WI., "Inside Nicaragua," June 29, 1986.

Peter A. Geniesse, The Post-Crescent, Appleton, WI, "Nicaraguans strode into democracy," March 4, 1990

Wikipedia, the free encyclopedia, "Daniel Ortega," June 1, 2015.

Julia Preston, New York Times, "Pope returns in Jubilation," Feb. 7, 1996.

CHAPTER TWELVE

Photo by Peter A. Geniesse
John Demjamjuk listens to testimony in 1987 in an Israeli courtroom where he was accused of being "Ivan the Terrible" at the Treblinka extermination camp in Nazi-occupied Poland.

"My father never hurt anyone. He doesn't even drink or smoke. He's a good man."
—John Demjamjuk's daughter.

CHAPTER TWELVE

'IVAN' DEMJAMJUK

1920-2012
Jerusalem 1987

For 17 years, John Demjamjuk lived in the Cleveland suburb of Seven Hills with his wife and three children. He had a good job, and apparently a good life. He was an UAW diesel engine mechanic for a nearby Ford auto plant.

He was born in 1920 in a farming village in Ukraine during tough times, came to the United States in 1952 and became a naturalized citizen in 1958.

Then one day in 1975 he was outed. His name showed up on a list of ethnic Ukrainians living in the U.S. suspected of collaborating with the Germans during the war. For the next 25 years he was called "Ivan the Terrible."

As his life story unfolded, Demjamjuk stood accused of war crimes as an accessory to the murder of 27,900 Jews at the Nazi extermination camp near Sobibor in occupied Poland.

Records show he was drafted into the Soviet Red Army in 1941, and after a battle in Eastern Crimea he was captured and became a German prisoner of war. He was moved to a Nazi German concentration camp for Soviet POWs. The camps were notorious for starving Soviet prisoners to death. Demjamjuk survived by volunteering to serve the Nazi German command.

In 1977 his U.S. citizenship was revoked on the basis that he had concealed his involvement with Nazi death camps on his immigration application. Israel later issued an extradition request for him to stand trial on Israeli soil. He was finally deported to Israel in 1986 and his two-year trial before the Jerusalem District Court opened that November.

That's when a group of American journalists, on a tour sponsored in part by the World Zionist Organization, got a front row seat on a Holocaust trial that was to linger for decades. There were 26 of us from 19 states, many of them Jews. Two of them were children of Holocaust survivors.

It was the biggest judicial news story in Israel since Adolf Eichmann stood trial in the 1960s. He was found guilty and was executed, the only time the death penalty had been carried out in Israel.

Demjanjuk sat dispassionately in court between two guards and his translator. His son, John Jr., a 21-year-old college student, watched the proceedings from a table behind his father. His two daughters and a grandchild looked on from the press gallery.

Each day the courtroom was jammed with spectators, many of whom were survivors or sons and daughters of survivors of the Holocaust. Each day the newspapers gave an updated account of the testimony.

The witnesses told of the deportation of the Jews from the Warsaw ghetto, the hunger, the beatings, the killings, the atrocities at the death camps. They then hysterically pointed to "Ivan the Terrible."

Demjanjuk listened to the testimony by way of a simultaneous translation on his headset. His American attorney, Marc O'Connor, and his Israeli counsel, Yoram Sheftel, questioned the witnesses. His children, born in the U.S. more than a decade after World War II, believed in their father's innocence. They were stunned by the testimony.

Irene Nishnic, 27, the mother of Demjanjuk's 15-month-old grandchild, told the *Jerusalem Post*: "My father has never hurt anyone. He has never beaten us or our mother. He doesn't even drink or smoke.

"He's a good man, a loving man."

"You have to know Yad Vashem to know what makes us tick," Ruben Dafni said. He's the director of Israel's Holocaust Museum.

"In our conscious, or in our subconscious, the national trauma is always with us," he added.

The Yad Vashem museum, visited by millions each year, is a grim, awesome testimony of man's inhumanity to man. It traces the rise of Nazism and the slaughter of a people. It contains 52 million documents and the names of three million known Jews who died in the Holocaust. Lining the walls are photos of concentration camps, of gruesome medical experiments, of gas chambers, of piles of corpses, of the living dead clinging to strands of barbed wire.

Six million Jews, including one and a half million children, were systematically exterminated over a six-year period in Europe. There were only seven million Jews on the continent at the time and 16 million throughout the world.

"No normal human being can fathom six million people dead," Dafni said. "It's the biggest tragedy that befell our people in its entire history."

On the floor of the windowless Memorial Hall at Yad Vashem are inlaid the names of the Nazi extermination camps, within the flickering glow of an everlasting flame. Somber ceremonies are held there each day. Two of our group, kin of Holocaust survivors, took part.

In 1987, more than four decades after the Holocaust, Israeli President Chaim Herzog paid his nation's first official visit to Germany. It was an act of conciliation, but not of forgiveness. He visited the Nazi death camp at Bergen-Belsen, the one he helped liberate in 1945 as an officer in the British army.

In dedicating a monument to the Holocaust, Herzog said, "The only ones who can forgive are the dead, and the living have no right to forget."

As the trial went on in Jerusalem, Demjanjuk was identified by 11 Holocaust survivors as "Ivan the Terrible," the notorious guard at the Treblinka extermination camp in Nazi occupied Poland. He was accused of committing murder and acts of extraordinary savage violence against camp prisoners in 1942-43.

He was convicted of committing crimes against humanity and sentenced to death by hanging on April 18, 1988. The court found Demjanjuk "unhesitatingly and with utter conviction" guilty of all charges. He was placed in solitary confinement during the appeals process.

That verdict was overturned by the Israeli Supreme Court in 1993, based on new evidence that "Ivan the Terrible" was probably another man, Ivan Marchenko.

Demjanjuk returned to his home in Ohio. In 1998 his citizenship was restored after a U.S. federal appeals court ruled that prosecutors had suppressed exculpatory evidence concerning his identity.

In 2001, with new evidence, Demjanjuk was charged once again, this time on the grounds that he had served as a guard at the Sobibor and Maidanek camps in Nazi occupied Poland and at the Flossenburg camp in Germany. Once again he became a stateless person in 2002.

His deportation again was ordered in 2005, but after exhausting his appeals in 2008 he still remained in the U.S., as no country would agree to accept him at that time. On April 2, 2009, it was announced that he would be deported to Germany where he would stand trial.

In a bid to disassociate from the nation's past, Germany began the policy of prosecuting prisoners of war from other nations whom the German Nazis made accessories to their crimes.

On May 11, Demjanjuk left his Cleveland home by ambulance, and was taken to the airport where he departed by plane, arriving in Germany the next morning. He was 89 years old and in poor health, suffering from leukemia, kidney and spinal problems and several types of gout.

Upon his arrival he was arrested and sent to Munich's Stadelheim prison. On July 13 he was formally charged with 27,900 counts of acting as an accessory to murder, one for each person who died at Sobibor during the time he was alleged to have served as guard.

On May 12, 2011, Demjanjuk was convicted of the charges and sentenced to five years in prison. After the conviction he was released pending the final verdict by the German Appellate Court. He lived at a German nursing home in Bad Feilnbach.

He died there on March 17, 2012, of natural causes at age 91, before his appeal could be heard. He was legally innocent.

He died a free man.

Resources:

Robert McFadden, New York Times, "John Demjanjuk, 91, dies," March 17, 2012.

Wikipedia, the free encyclopedia, "John Demjanjuk," June 7, 2015

Peter A. Geniesse, The Post-Crescent, Appleton, WI., "The Holocaust Trauma," April 16, 1987.

CHAPTER THIRTEEN

Photo by Peter A. Geniesse

Israeli Prime Minister Yitzhak Rabin addresses a group of U.S. journalists visiting Jerusalem about his peace efforts in the fall of 1987. He was a Nobel Peace Prize recipient in 1994 and the following year he was assassinated.

"I believe the only way to bring about peace between an Arab country and Israel is by direct, bilateral negotiations."
—Yitzhak Rabin

CHAPTER THIRTEEN

YITZHAK RABIN

1922-1995
Jerusalem   1987

"Atheism," the old man growled. "It's the only way to peace."

His lips were quivering as he spouted a litany of wars, from Old Testament times to the Crusades to Northern Ireland to the Middle East.

"They were all fought in the name of God," he said.

If there were no religion, he said, there'd be peace.

He was an eastern European Jew who had immigrated to the United States. He returns to Israel every other year to refresh his ethnic –if not his religious – roots.

He was my seatmate on an El Al flight from Tel Aviv to New York.

"Shalom," he said, as he shook my hand.

Most people say "shalom" here in the holy city. Many, however, say "salaam," the Arabic salutation.

Whatever they say, Jerusalem is not a place at peace.

For five thousand years, the city has been a battleground – for Canaanites, for Jebusites, for Babyalonians, Jews, Romans, Greeks, Christians and Arabs. It's been leveled, converted and pillaged. Holy sites have been destroyed and resurrected. A temple becomes a church which is turned into a mosque.

Here at the wellspring of the world's three great monotheistic religions, strife reigns, not peace.

The waves of war in the 20th century started with the War of Independence in 1948. The Israel Defense Forces were called upon to fight in four more major conflicts within the next three decades with its Arab neighbors.

In May of 1948, the I.D.F. repelled the invasions by Arab armies from Egypt, Jordan, Iraq, Syria, Lebanon and Saudi Arabia. A year later, armistice agreements were signed and partition boundaries were firmed.

Eight years later, in October 1956, in the Sinai Campaign, Egypt blocked Israel shipping from the Straits of Tiran. I.D.F. captured Egyptian bases in Gaza and Sinai. Six months later Israel returned the territories to Egypt.

In June 1967, in the "Six Day War," Egypt again closed shipping and paid the price. Israel destroyed the Egyptian air force on the ground. The I.D.F. repelled Jordan on the east and Syria on the north. Israel took control of Judea-Samaria, Gaza, Sinai and Golan Heights.

In the spring of 1969, in the War of Attrition, Egypt started shelling across the Suez Canal and the Israeli air force attacked its positions. Four months later, the war ended with a cease fire.

In October 1973, in the Yom Kipper War, Egypt and Syria launched simultaneous attacks on Israel. The I.D.F. repelled the invasions, and a U.S.-sponsored cease-fire ended two weeks of fighting.

The Camp David peace agreements signed by Egypt's Anwar Sadat and Israel's Menachem Begin and witnessed by U.S. President Jimmy Carter in March 1979 held hopes for a lasting peace among the Arab neighbors.

Yitzhak Rabin was Minister of Defense at the time. He was a warrior but he was tiring of perpetual armed conflicts just to assure the survival of Israel. He laid out his peace program at a 1987 press conference with visiting American journalists.

"I believe the only way to bring about peace between an Arab country and Israel is by direct, bilateral negotiations," he said. "We cannot impose peace on the Arabs, the Arabs cannot impose peace on us, and the superpowers cannot impose peace either."

Rabin noted that Israel's military success "has been blown out of proportion" but he said the country's security has to ride on more than its reputation.

Israel, bordered by foes on three sides and more enemies within its borders, does not expect love from its neighbors. But it demands respect.

"We would like to deter the enemy by proving that he cannot achieve his goals," Rabin said, "that he'd be clobbered if he tried."

He added, "We're in good shape, but we cannot risk the security of this country on hopes and expectations. Our defense policy is aimed to prevent war."

A healthy perception of the balance of power is what keeps the uneasy peace in the region, the defense minister said. If the Arabs perceive they have the edge, they'll try again.

He saw threats on the borders from Arab states, Syria in particular, and in the territories from Palestinian terrorism.

But he noted, "Syria alone is no match for Israel." Still, he added, "I hope the Syrian leaders are capable of weighing strengths."

What worried Rabin the most was the prospect of peace among Muslim nations. "A united Arab world is bad for Israel," he said. "We don't want anyone winning the Iran-Iraq war."

That war, at the time in its sixth year at a cost of $100 billion, has distracted and divided the Muslim world and has taken some of the Arab pressure from Israel, Rabin said.

But terrorism, internal, on the frontiers and abroad, had Israeli officials concerned. Rabin noted there were 50 terrorist organizations in the region.

"We know we are on top of the list of all of them," he said.

Yitzhak Rabin was born in Jerusalem in 1922 to parents who had come from Europe on the third wave of Jewish immigration to Palestine. He grew up in Tel Aviv in a Labor-Zionist household. When he was 13, he joined a socialist-Zionist group and five years later he immigrated to the United States where he joined the Poale Zion party.

He returned to Israel in 1941, was recruited by Moshe Dayan for the Palmach section of the Haganah and started a military career that lasted three decades.

In October, 1945, Rabin was in charge of planning an operation for the release of interned Jewish illegal immigrants. He was arrested and detained by the British Mandate for five months.

During the 1948 Arab-Israeli war, Rabin directed operations in Jerusalem and fought the Egyptian army in the Negev. The following year he was named to the Israeli delegation's armistice talks with Egypt on the Island of Rhodes which ended the war.

In 1964, he was appointed chief of staff of the Israel Defense Forces by Levi Eshkol, who had replaced David Ben-Gurion. Under his command, the I.D.F. achieved victory over Egypt, Syria and Jordan in the Six-Day War of 1967.

In 1968, Rabin was named ambassador to the United States. During his five-year stay, the U.S. became the major weapon supplier of Israel. He also succeeded in lifting the U.S. embargo on the F-4 Phantom fighter jets.

Rabin succeeded Golda Meir as Prime Minister of Israel in April 1974. At the beginning of his term, he signed the Sinai Interim Agreement between Israel and Egypt. Both countries declared that the conflict between them and in the Middle East shall not be resolved by military force but by peaceful means.

That agreement followed Henry Kissinger's shuttle diplomacy and a threatened "reassessment" of the United States' regional policy and its relations with Israel. The agreement was an important step toward the Camp David Accords of 1978 and the peace treaty with Egypt in 1979.

Operation Entebbe was the most dramatic event during Rabin's first term. On his orders, the I.D.F. performed a long-range undercover raid to rescue passengers of an airliner hijacked by militants and flown to Idi Amin's Uganda.

Rabin was a member of the Knesset and sat on the Foreign Affairs and Defense Committees and he served a second term as prime minister in the 1990s.

The Oslo Accords, penned after secret negotiations in Norway, were a set of agreements between the government of Israel and the Palestine Liberation Organization, signed in Washington, D.C. on Sept. 13, 1993, in the presence of PLO chairman Yasser Arafat, Israeli Prime Minister Yitzhak Rabin and U.S. President Bill Clinton.

The early "peace process" results were encouraging. The PLO recognized the State of Israel and Israel recognized the PLO as the representative of the Palestinian people.

It created the Palestinian Authority and its limited governance over parts of the West Bank and the Gaza Strip and it acknowledged that the PLO was now Israel's partner in permanent status negotiations.

It set the stage for negotiations on key issues: the borders of Israel and Palestine, Israel settlements, the status of Jerusalem, the question of Israel's military presence in the territories and the Palestinian right of return.

In 1994, Rabin, Arafat and Israeli Foreign Minister Shimon Peres received the Nobel Peace Prize "for their efforts to create peace in the Middle East."

It didn't last. The Oslo process ended after the failure of the Camp David Summit in 2000 and the outbreak of the Second Intifada.

At the start, Rabin had been assailed by national religious conservatives and Likud party leaders for his support of the "peace process." Despite his extensive service in the Israeli military, he was disparaged personally by those who perceived the Oslo Accords as an attempt to forfeit the occupied territories.

Likud leader Benjamin Netanyahu accused Rabin's government of being "removed from Jewish tradition and Jewish values." He addressed Oslo opposition rallies where posters portrayed Rabin in a Nazi SS uniform or being in the crosshairs of a sniper. Rabin accused Netanyahu of provoking violence.

On Nov. 4, 1995, Rabin spoke at a rally in support of "peace process" of the Oslo Accords at the Kings of Israel Square in Tel Aviv.

After the rally as Rabin walked down the steps of city hall to his car, an assassin fired three shots at close range. Rabin was rushed to a hospital where he died 40 minutes later.

In Rabin's pocket was a blood-stained sheet of paper with the lyrics to the well-known Israeli song "Shir LaShalom," Song of Peace, which was sung at the rally. The words dwell on the impossibility of bringing a dead person back to life and, therefore, the need for peace.

The assassin, Yigal Amir, a law student at Bar-Ilan University, opposed Rabin's peace initiative, fearing it would deny Jews "their biblical heritage which they had reclaimed by establishing settlements" on the West Bank.

Rabin's funeral took place on Nov. 6 at the Mount Herzl Cemetery in Jerusalem, and was attended by hundreds of world leaders, including President Clinton and more than 80 heads of state.

Amir was sentenced to life in prison.

Resources:

Peter A. Geniesse, The Post-Crescent, Appleton, Wis., "Spying," April 13, 1967.

Wikipedia, the free encyclopedia, "Oslo Accords," "Rabin Assassination," June 9, 2015.

CHAPTER FOURTEEN

Photo by Peter A. Geniesse

Lt. Col. Raanan Gissen, a strategic analyst for the Israel Defense Forces, told visiting American journalists in Jerusalem in 1987 that Israel's security demands that It can never let down its guard.

"I am neither a traitor nor a spy. I only wanted the world to know what was happening."
—Mordechai Vanunu

CHAPTER FOURTEEN

MORDECHAI VANUNU

1954-
Ashkelon, Israel   1986

Few knew the name of the American Jew who spied for Israel and received a life sentence in a U.S. prison back in 1987.

Jonathon Jay Pollard, 32, a former U.S. civilian intelligence analyst, sold a huge batch of classified documents to Israeli intelligence officials in the United States in 1985.

"No one on the political level knew of the Pollard case," Israeli Defense Minister Yitzhak Rabin said.

The "Pollard Affair" made headlines in the U.S. but it was business as usual in Israel. "Spying is an international sport," one Israeli official said. "Some countries have spies in the skies and others send people to spy.

"We couldn't be successful without covert operations," he added. "Intelligence is better than fighting a war."

About the same time in Israel another spy story was unfolding. This one, when revealed, would send vibrations throughout the Western world.

His name is Mordechai Vanunu. He's either a whistleblower, a traitor, a spy, or "the preeminent hero of the nuclear era." He was tried in secret by an Israeli court, and was sentenced to 18 years in prison, serving 11 years in solitary confinement.

The Israeli government didn't want his story to get out. It was about the production of nuclear weapons at a well-guarded, secret facility in the Negev Desert, not far from the city of Dimona.

The story did get out, however. In September, 1986, the British *Sunday Times* published the details of Israel's nuclear program, including photos provided by Vanunu.

To this day, information about the facility remains highly classified. Israel refuses to disclose details, citing an intentional policy of "nuclear ambiguity." It neither acknowledges nor denies that it possesses nuclear weapons.

Mordechai Vanunu was born in Marrakesh, Morocco, in 1954, into an orthodox Jewish family. Nine years later, sensing a rise in anti-semitic sentiment, the family emigrated to Israel, settling in Beersheba.

In October, 1971, Vanunu was conscripted into the Israel Defense Forces. Two years later, he was stationed on the Golan Heights and saw action in the 1973 Yom Kippur War. He was honorably discharged in 1974, and enrolled at Tel Aviv University and studied physics before dropping out due to financial constraints.

He was 22 when he applied for a job at the Negev Nuclear Research Center, and after intensive training, he was employed as a nuclear plant technician. He also enrolled at Ben-Gurion University of the Negev in Beersheba. He traveled throughout Europe and spent three months in the U.S. and Canada.

He became openly critical of the Israeli government, joining a group called "Movement for the Advancement of Peace" and campaigning for equal rights for Arab Israelis. His security file at the Negev Nuclear Research Center noted that Vanunu displayed "left-wing and pro-Arab beliefs."

He was interrogated at the facility's security office and was warned against divulging any unauthorized information.

Vanunu quit his job in October, 1985, due to repeated efforts by his superiors to transfer him to tasks that were less sensitive.

He loved to travel and made several trips to the Far East, to Thailand, to Russia and ended up in Australia, where he converted to Christianity, joining the Anglican Church. He met a free-lance journalist who encouraged him to go public with his inside story of Israel's nuclear program.

After failing to interest *Newsweek*, the journalist contacted the British *Sunday Times.* Vanunu flew to London, and in violation of his non-disclosure agreement, he revealed to the *Sunday Times* his knowledge of the Israeli nuclear program, including the photographs he had secretly taken at the Dimona site.

The *Sunday Times* was wary of being duped, especially in light of the recent "Hitler Diaries" hoax. The newspaper insisted on verifying Vanunu's story with leading nuclear weapon experts. They agreed that Vanunu's story was factual and correct.

Vanunu was frustrated with the delay. He approached a rival newspaper, the tabloid *Sunday Mirror*, with the story idea, unaware that its owner, Robert Maxwell, was an agent for Israeli intelligence services. Maxwell tipped off the Israeli Embassy about Vanunu's story.

The Israeli government decided to kidnap Vanunu by using the classic "honey trap" operation. An American tourist, called "Cindy," joined Vanunu on a romantic flight to Rome. It coincided with the arrival of "INS Noga," an Israeli surveillance ship, which was moored off the Italian coast near La Specia.

Once in Rome, Vanunu was accosted by three Israeli Mossad agents who overpowered him and injected him with a paralyzing drug. He was taken by ambulance to the coast, transferred to a speed boat and placed aboard the INS Noga, all in total secrecy.

On Oct. 6, the day after the *Sunday Times* published Vanunu interview, he was on a ship anchored off the coast of Israel, between Tel Aviv and Haifa. Vanunu was taken ashore, in custody, and questioned by Mossad interrogators.

Vanunu was put on trial, held in secret, in the Jerusalem District Court. He was not permitted contact with the media.

On March 28, 1988, he was convicted of treason and espionage and sentenced to 18 years of imprisonment. The Israeli government refused to release the transcript of the court case until 1999, after a legal challenge.

The death penalty in Israel is restricted to special circumstances, and only two executions have ever taken place. The option of extrajudicial execution was considered but rejected because "Jews don't do that to other Jews."

Vanunu served his 18-year sentence at Shikma Prison in Ashkelon. He spent more than 11 years in solitary confinement, allegedly out of concern that he might reveal more Israeli nuclear secrets.

However, critics say that Vanunu had no additional information that would pose a security threat to Israel. The government's real motivation, they say, is a desire to avoid political embarrassment as well as financial complications for itself and allies, such as the United States.

By not acknowledging possession of nuclear weapons, Israel avoids a U.S. legal prohibition on funding countries which proliferate weapons of mass destruction. Such an admission would prevent Israel from receiving more than $2 billion each year in military and other aid from Washington.

Nick and Mary Eoloff, political activists from St. Paul, Minnesota, first read about Vanunu's case in The Progressive in 1995.

"I read his story and I thought it was out of the Dark Ages," Mary Eoloff said. "To keep someone in a six-foot by nine-foot cell is unreal."

Nick Eoloff added, "He had been in isolation longer than any person in the Western world. Just the brutality of that is very moving."

The couple started writing to Mordechai and actively working on a campaign to free him.

"From our perspective, nothing could ever justify the use of nuclear weapons," Nick Eoloff said. "He's anti-nuclear and we're anti-nuclear, so we've got that common bond."

The Eoloffs were Quakers and Green Party supporters, as well as leaders in Pax Christi International, a Catholic peace and social justice movement. I met the couple at a Pax Christi conference in New York City in 2003 and joined their campaign to free Vanunu.

Mary co-founded the "Peace Studies Task Force," published a textbook on conscientious objection and taught non-violence to high school students throughout the Twin Cities region.

The couple petitioned the U.S. Congress to intervene in Vanunu's case and to pressure Israel to free him. "It all proved fruitless," Nick said. "We felt like we were getting nowhere. We wanted to help this human being."

So they entertained the thought of adopting the 44-year-old prisoner of conscience. They figured Israel someday would like to get rid of him, and if he were adopted, Vanunu could become a U.S. citizen and be released from prison.

It was a difficult process going through the courts, but with the assistance of a friendly Minnesota judge the papers went through and Nick and Mary were on their way to Israel see their adoptive son.

"We just showed up at the prison and said, 'Hi, we're Mordechai's parents,'" Nick said.

Since that day in February, 1998, the couple visited Vanunu 13 times. They also told their story on a British BBC documentary entitled "Israel's Secret Weapon" which was aired world-wide on June 29, 2003.

Nick Eoloff died on May 24, 2014, at the age of 84. His wife, Mary, died five months later. She was 82. They are survived by six children, 14 grandchildren, one great-grandchild and one adopted son in Israel.

Mordechai Vanunu was released from prison on April 21, 2004, after serving the 18-year term. But he's still not free.

"I am neither a traitor nor a spy," he said that day. "I only wanted the world to know what was happening."

Since he left prison, he has been staying at St. George's Cathedral in Jerusalem. He receives visitors and has defied the conditions of his release by giving interviews to foreign journalists.

He is not allowed to leave Israel. He can't come within 500 meters of the border. No cell phones, no Internet, no contact with foreigners. He is still bound by his non-disclosure agreement.

Israeli authorities say these restrictions are necessary because of fear of his spreading further state secrets. On Oct. 11, 2010, Vanunu's appeal to rescind the restrictions and allow him to leave Israel and speak to foreigners was denied by the Israeli Supreme Court.

Vanunu repeatedly has violated the restrictions, and has served jail time for those offenses. Amnesty International came to his defense after one incarceration. "If Mordechai Vanunu is imprisoned again, we will declare him to be a prisoner of conscience and call for his immediate and unconditional release."

Vanunu has been nominated for the Nobel Peace Prize every year since 1987. In 2009 he asked the committee to remove his name from consideration.

"I cannot be part of a list of laureates that includes Shimon Peres, the president of Israel," he wrote. "He established and developed the atomic weapon program at Dimona.

"He was the man who ordered my kidnaping in Rome in 1986, and for the secret trial and sentencing of me as a spy and traitor, and for my 18 years in prison."

Vanunu declared, "I say no to any nomination as long as I'm not free, that is, as long as I am still forced to be in Israel.

"What I want is freedom, and only freedom."

The Negev Nuclear Research Center is still in business a half-century after its birth. The complex was constructed in secret, with

French assistance, in 1958. To maintain secrecy, French officials were told the reactor tank was part of a desalination plant bound for Latin America.

The cost of the facility was estimated at $80 million, paid for in part by "Israel's friends around the world," according to Shimon Peres' 1995 memoir.

The Dimona reactor became active in the early 1960s. When the U.S. intelligence community discovered the purpose of the site, the U.S. government demanded that Israel agree to international inspections.

The U.S. inspectors eventually informed the U.S. government that their inspections were useless, due to Israeli restrictions on what areas of the facility they could inspect.

By 1969, the U.S. believed that Israel might have a nuclear weapon. Inspections were ended that year.

In January, 2012, media reports indicated that the Israel Atomic Energy Commission had decided to shut down the reactor, at least temporarily. The site's vulnerability to attack from Iran was cited as the main reason for the decision.

Resources:

Claire Shaeffer-Duffy, National Catholic Reporter, "Adopting Mordechai Vanunu, Nov. 24, 2000.

Michael Jacobson, Paynesville Press, "Free Mordechai," Jan. 18, 2003.

U.S. Campaign to Free Mordechai Vanunu, April 22, 2004.

Wikipedia, the free encyclopedia, "Negev Nuclear Reserch Center," June 15, 2015.

Star Tribune, St. Paul, MN., "Peace Activist Mary Eoloff," Oct. 13, 2014.

BBC World Service Transcript, "Israel's Secret Weapon," June 29, 2003.

Chapter Fifteen

Photo by Peter A. Geniesse
Three young "Pioneers" pose in front of a poster of Cuba's revolutionaries Che Guevara and Fidel Castro at Isla de Juventud, home to thousands of students from Third World nations in 1988.

"He who betrays the poor, betrays Christ. I think one can be a Marxist without ceasing to be Christian."
–Fidel Castro

CHAPTER FIFTEEN

'FIDELISMO' CASTRO RUZ

1926 —
Havana, Cuba   1988

David Salsero flattened his nose against the window of the Eastern Airlines 727 charter jet. At 3 a.m. the lights of Miami suddenly twinkled through the clouds revealing miles and miles of urban sprawl.

"*Mira, mama,*" the excited 10-year-old whispered to his mother. His sister, Leybel, 12, told him to hush and sit straight.

They were Cuban refugees, dressed in their Sunday best. Their father and grandfather had spent years in Fidel Castro's prisons. But now they were free to start anew in the Havana of the north.

They wanted to shout for joy as the plane landed at Miami's International Airport, just 35 minutes away from their communist homeland. But they didn't dare.

Ten families of political prisoners were aboard, a total of 31 people. They were outnumbered, however, by left-leaning Americans returning to the U.S. after touring Cuba. Those Americans, they were told, wouldn't share their enthusiasm in leaving Cuba for freedom in the states.

The Americans queued up for customs, carefully selecting the lines in front of non-Latin-looking officials. Cubans in Miami are suspicious of travelers to Cuba.

After two hours, the Cuban refugees were released. More than 300 Miami Cubans awaited behind the barriers to welcome the latest arrivals. Emotions that had been welling up inside broke loose. Kinfolk and some former cellmates shared hugs, kisses, cheers and tears.

They were home in Miami, the second largest Cuban city in the world. Here they could be anti-Castro like everyone else.

Bruno Salas, 56, served 21 years in Cuban prisons on charges of being a CIA conduit. He was accused of sending intelligence to the CIA and was sentenced to 30 years. He and 23 other political prisoners were freed in 1987 as sort of a goodwill gesture from Castro.

Salas was at the airport to welcome the new exiles, some of whom he knew from early counter-revolutionary activities and from prison. He worked for Radio Marti, the Voice of America's controversial voice for Cuba, based in Miami.

Most of the Cuban refugees had kinfolk in Miami. David and Leybel's aunt arrived in Miami with the Mariel boatlift. Their grandfather, José Manuel Caso, 71, spent 16 years in prison, and their father, Juan Salsero, served 14 years of a 30-year sentence.

Both said they were imprisoned "for talking against Castro." Upon further questioning, they admitted guns and counter-revolutionary sabotage were involved.

More than a million Cubans have settled in in the U.S. since Castro came to power. The first wave in the early 1960s included land barons, big businessmen and professionals, those who had the most to lose under socialism. They packed their bags and left their estates untended, assuming they would be back home within six months.

Some tried to return, forming Brigade 2106, which was shot down at the Bay of Pigs in the spring of 1961.

Another generation of Cubans fled to the U.S. in the Freedom Flotilla two decades later. As many as 125,000 people, mostly young and unskilled, came by air and by sea. They were known as *Marielitos*, from the name of the port near Havana.

Many reportedly had been in Cuban prisons and mental institutions, and more than a few ended up behind bars in the U.S.

While most Cubans favored Castro's revolution, and felt they were better off than they were in the 1950s, the waiting list for Cubans wishing to leave the island nation was substantial. The U.S. Interest

Section in Havana estimated that the flow of refugees would top 20,000 a year if the gates were opened.

Back in 1988, Fidel Castro was 61 and had ruled the country for nearly 30 years. Ever since New Year's Day in 1959, when he marched triumphantly onto Havana, Fidel has called the shots. His brother Raul was vice president and next in line, but his name was hardly a household chant.

Cubans had come to realize that someday Fidel just might not be around. Without question, the charismatic leader would be missed. He was an attorney by education, a guerrilla fighter by necessity, a father figure to millions and a Third World force to be reckoned with.

In Havana they called him Fidel. In Miami they called him Castro.

Fidel's revolution traces its roots back to July 26, 1953, the 100th anniversary of the birth of José Martí, independence hero and father of the country.

Fidel and 123 young revolutionaries attacked the Moncada barracks in Santiago, believing Cuban dictator Fulgencio Batista's troops would be vulnerable during the national feast day. They weren't. Half of Fidel's troops were killed and the others, including Fidel and his brother Raul were captured and imprisoned on the Isle of Pines, Batista's massive complex for political and common criminals.

But while the attack proved to be a disaster, it gave birth to the revolutionary movement, the "*26 de Julio.*" It made the unknown Fidel a daring folk hero among the peasants and even some middle class folks who wanted the corrupt Batista regime overthrown.

In 1955, with Batista facing an election in an increasingly hostile nation, Fidel and his men were given a general amnesty as a gesture of good will. Fidel fled to Mexico, got together with Ernesto "Che" Guevara and put together a band of guerrilla fighters.

In early December of 1956, with financial and moral support growing for the revolution at home, Fidel and his band of 81 men boarded the "Granma," a decrepit yacht, and landed in the Oriente Province of Cuba. They set up camp in the Sierra Maestra mountains and Fidel's name and claim on the country started to reverberate throughout the province.

The Batista regime was seen as so corrupt and his enemies so numerous that Fidel easily captured the allegiance of the countryside. Within two years his guerrilla and peasant army had gained the upper hand.

Batista fled to the Dominican Republic when his army's loyalty faded. He later moved to Portugal and died in Spain in 1973.

Fidel, at age 31, was at the helm in Cuba on New Year's Day, 1959.

At first, almost all Cubans saw Fidel as a hero. Even in the United States, he was viewed as a liberator. But when he pushed through land reform, nationalized the banks and some industries, wealthy Cubans and American investors began crying "communist."

In the first year, some $800 million in U.S. investments were nationalized. In January 1961, the U.S. severed diplomatic ties and Cuba turned to the Soviet Union. Anti-Castro Cubans flocked to the United States, with most of them settling in Miami.

Then came the Cuban missile crisis in October 1962, when the world was face-to-face with nuclear war. The Soviets blinked and the United States said it wouldn't invade Cuba if Russia removed the missiles.

That, however, didn't close the books on efforts to overthrow Castro. Many of the blockades, sabotage, schemes to kill Castro and aborted plans for new invasions have been directly linked to the CIA and the Miami exiles.

"Those in privileged positions will now be less privileged, but those who are hard up will radically improve their situation," Fidel said as his government embarked on the first socialistic experiment in the Western Hemisphere.

Before the revolution, 15 percent of the people controlled half of the nation's wealth. Nine percent of the farmers owned two-thirds of the land. Half of the children had no access to school, and illiteracy in rural areas was 42 percent.

Basic foods then were rationed so no one would go hungry. Huge landholdings were broken up. Government housing clusters replaced the "*bohios*," the palm-thatched huts common in the countryside. Fidel issued a call for 100,000 "teachers" to attack rural illiteracy, and within six months the illiteracy rate was cut in half.

Medical care was next. The need was especially great due to the exodus of Havana physicians to the U.S. Cuba opened medical schools and produced 40,000 doctors over three decades. The goal was met to have one doctor for every 150 families.

In less than 30 years, Cuba and Castro had turned around more than a century of poverty and privilege.

"The revolution has met the basic needs of all," said Wayne Smith, chief of the U.S. Interests Section in Havana in 1981. "There is no one who goes hungry."

To writer Robert Louis Stevenson, it was called "Treasure Island." To dictator Fulgencio Batista, it was a holding tank for thousands of political and common criminals. To Fidel Castro, it was to become a Third World campus to sow the seeds of revolution for emerging nations.

What once was known as the Isle of Pines, an agricultural pocket in the Caribbean just a short hop from Havana, Castro renamed "*Isla de Juventud*."

In 1988 it was home to 22,000 students from 36 Third World countries, mostly in Africa and Asia. The majority of those nations had recent revolutions or movements toward independence. All either had socialistic governments or were in transition toward them.

Nowhere else in the world were there so many potential national leaders forging friendships while honing their skills and ideologies.

Cuba, once a relatively insignificant sugar and pleasure fiefdom for the United States, emerged under Castro as the leader of the Third World. It sent thousands of technicians, teachers and physicians to developing countries. It also has sent thousands of soldiers to fight in such places as Angola.

And on that "Island of Youth," Cuba trained thousands of Latin, African and Asian youths to lead their own countries into the 21st century.

Castro was 26 when he arrived at that island prison in 1953 following the "26 de Julio" attack on the Moncada barracks in Santiago. When he and his men were granted amnesty two years later, the island classroom already had fomented the framework for a revolution.

The island held a massive prison, labeled "*Presidio Modelo*," built to the design of the federal penitentiary at Joliet, Illinois. There were four giant circular bastions, each with 455 cells for prisoners.

On the eve of the revolution, Batista ordered two prisoners to each cell and 3,600 were housed in the massive complex.

Castro then used the prison for his purposes, locking up counter-revolutionaries. In 1967, the bars were removed and plans were in place to convert part of the prison into a museum. Half of the complex was turned into a "Pioneers' Palace," a vocational-technical school for thousands of foreign teenagers.

In 1978, Castro opened his "grand communist university for students around the world." Cuba constructed individual campuses, with modern dormitories, classrooms and science labs for 36 Third World nations. Students from such countries as North Korea, Angola, Nicaragua, Uganda and Mozambique spent up to six years completing high school and technical training.

Each country picked as many as 600 of its best students, boys and girls, between the ages of 14 and 20, to complete their education, free of charge.

The experiment didn't last, however, and long before 2015 the island had become a tourist haven, with dormitories converted to housing for a population of 100,000.

Cuba, often accused by the U.S. of exporting revolution around the world, and especially in Latin America, had a substantial presence in more than a dozen countries. It sent thousands of workers and technicians, under labor contracts, to Czechoslovakia, East Germany, Bulgaria and Hungry.

Cubans abroad were even more in evidence in Third World nations, and most of them were in Africa as soldiers, teachers and medical people. In Angola, 40,000 Cuban troops were fighting to keep the Marxists in power. Castro's "economic technicians" were in Ethiopia, Libya and Mozambique, among other African nations.

Cuba also had troops in Iraq and South Yemen, and substantial presence in Nicaragua during the early stages of its revolution.

During the 1980s, Castro and Cuba occupied center stage in the Third World.

I joined the 10th annual United Church of Christ two-week study seminar in Cuba in January, 1988, to see for myself what Castro had wrought. The U.S. allowed clergymen and journalists to visit the forbidden planet. So, as editor, I signed press passes for three Wisconsinites who were laymen and joined them in their adventure.

We conducted more than two dozen wide-ranging interviews with Cuban officials as well as regular citizens. We visited prisons, schools and churches and even Ernest Hemmingway's hangouts. I interviewed his fishing buddy for "Old Man and the Sea."

We listened, some of the time, to Castro's four-hour diatribe against the imperialistic Yankees before tens of thousands of cheering Cubans at Jose Marti Square. We watched along the *malecón* as Soviet freighters entered the Havana harbor.

There's no question that some of the events were orchestrated. The prison visit, for example, included a variety show and a sing-along with the inmates. The stop by the neighborhood Committee for the Defense of the Revolution included rum and roses for all.

But I was free to go anywhere. I walked the streets of Havana at midnight, took buses 10 miles or more into the countryside, talked to U.S. officials at the "Interests Section," and even interviewed a Cuban dissident by phone. Nowhere did I feel watched. I raised the hackles on some Cuban officials with "insolent" questions but they answered, or ducked the question.

Since our group was mostly comprised of Presbyterian and UCC pastors, we had an inside connection with José Carneado, the "atheist Christian" who headed the ruling Communist Party's office of religious affairs. It was two years after Frei Betto's book, "Fidel and Religion," hit the stands. The Brazilian friar and liberation theologian's book sold 500,000 copies in Cuba to become the nation's all-time best seller.

Castro, who was baptized Catholic and was educated by the Christian Brothers and Jesuits, had converted the nation to "*Fidelismo*." But he had second thoughts about Christianity when he noted that priests in Nicaragua had formed Christian Base Communities, had opted for the poor and had supported the revolution there.

At the start of his revolution, he admonished the Catholic hierarchy for siding with the upper classes. "He who betrays the poor, betrays Christ," Castro said.

"I think one can be a Marxist without ceasing to be Christian," he told Frei Betto.

I spoke to at least a half-dozen church leaders in Cuba, both Catholic and Protestant, and they agreed that "God and the revolution" had done great things for the poor in Cuba.

The blind see and the lame walk, they said.

Raúl Castro sat in for his big brother when Fidel went to the hospital for colon cancer surgery on July 31, 2006. But age had taken its toll, and his recuperation was slow. Fidel was 80 when he stepped aside as Cuban president after 50 years in office.

Raúl, the youngest of three Castro brothers, was Fidel's right-hand man ever since the aborted revolutionary attack on the Moncada barracks in Santiago in 1953. He was 22 at the time. He served as Cuba's Defense Minister for more than a half-century.

Raúl officially became president of Cuba on Feb. 24, 2008, and was re-elected by the Council of State in 2013.

Cuba's Communist government had restricted religious worship and promoted atheism, but an opening came in 1996 when Fidel visited Pope John Paul II at the Vatican. The pope returned the favor by visiting Cuba two years later. Pope Benedict XVI also visited Cuba in 2012.

Cuban bishops then received permits to build the first new churches on the island since the 1959 revolution.

The Vatican and Cuba celebrated 80 years of diplomatic relations. The Vatican had long opposed the United States' sanctions against the island nation.

Raúl Castro met with U.S. President Barak Obama in an historical encounter at a regional summit in Panama, which led to 18 months of secret negotiations. That resulted in the announcement of détente by both presidents in December 2014.

Obama, in announcing that the U.S. would resume diplomatic ties with Cuba, credited Pope Francis as being the critical player. He said the pope helped jump-start the diplomacy with personal letters and also by allowing the Vatican to be used for a secret meeting between diplomats from both countries.

In May 2015, Cuban President Raúl Castro visited Pope Francis at the Vatican and praised the Argentine pontiff for helping to broker the diplomatic breakthrough between Cuba and the U.S.

Raul promised a warm welcome for Pope Francis when he arrived in Cuba in September before visiting the United States.

"I promised to go to all of his Masses, and with satisfaction," Raul said. He added that he had read all of the pontiff's speeches and commentaries "and if the pope continues this way, I will go back to praying and go back to the church."

Resources:

Jim Yardley, The New York Times: "Raul Castro meets Pope Francis," May 10, 2015.

Peter A. Geniesse, The Post-Crescent, Appleton, WI: "What Castro has wrought," Feb. 7, 1988

Wikipedia, the free encyclopedia: "Fidel Castro," June 17, 2015.

Voice of America, Reuters: "A Castro Son Rises in Cuba," June 17, 2015.

CHAPTER SIXTEEN

Photo by Peter A. Geniesse

The "Unknown Slave" statue blows a conch for freedom in front of the presidential palace in Port-au-Prince. Haiti won it independence in 1803 but never had free elections until Jean-Bertrand Aristide was elected almost two centuries later.

"Today may the Haitian people end exiles and coups d'etat while peacefully moving from social exclusion to inclusion."
–Jean-Bertrand Aristide

CHAPTER SIXTEEN

JEAN-BERTRAND ARISTIDE

1953 –
Port-au- Prince, Haiti   1993

"This is crazy," said the OAS observer.

"This is Haiti," said the young Haitian translator.

Antoine Szmery, just hours after embracing the Rev. Jesse Jackson in his appeal for an end to human rights violations, was arrested and jailed. Many feared it was a death sentence. Six months earlier, his brother George was gunned down in his office by a military squad. Antoine escaped.

The two brothers, wealthy Palestine merchants who had lived in Haiti for most of their lives, bankrolled exiled President Jean-Bertrand Aristide's campaign. They put up $600,000 and a bulletproof vest to help the slum-raised priest heed the cries of the poor.

Aristide, who survived three assassination attempts during the campaign, won 67 percent of the vote among 10 candidates in December 1990. Nine months later he was ousted by a military coup. More than 3,000 "*Lavalas*," Aristide supporters, were killed in the wake of the coup.

Szmery's charges? He had misplaced his driver's license.

The world community vigorously condemned the human rights violations in Haiti. The United Nations and the Organization of American States imposed economic sanctions and insisted that democracy be restored, that the military terror cease and that a team of outside observers monitor the political ills of the hemisphere's poorest country.

Yet the illegal arrests, torture and killings continued.

The U.S.-based Lawyer Committee for Human Rights compiled a chronical of political abuses in Haiti. It concluded: "Haiti is a human rights nightmare where the most fundamental freedoms are violated and where the violators enjoy virtual impunity."

Jesse Jackson spoke at the church that was Father Aristide's parish before he became a presidential candidate. It was there, three years earlier, that the military opened fire, killing 14, but missing Aristide. Jackson made an appeal for an end to violence – on both sides.

"The arrests must end. The necklacing must end," he said. Necklacing, or *"Pere Lebrun,"* was a retaliatory measure by the people who executed members of the feared *"Tonton Macoute"* in the streets with gasoline-charged flaming tires about their necks.

"There must be a new Haiti, a new U.S. policy, and 'Ti-de' (Aristide) will return," Jackson said.

Aristide served only nine months in office before the bloody military *coup d'etat*, led by Army General Raoul Cédras, on Sept. 29, 1991.

His agenda as president thrilled the poor and threatened the elite, a small privileged class who controlled the military. Aristide "retired" several generals, including the army's commander in chief, who were accused of human rights violations.

He banned the emigration of many wealthy Haitians until their bank accounts had been examined. And he brought to trial several *Tontons-Macoute* who had not fled the country.

After addressing the United Nations in New York on Sept. 28, he returned triumphantly to Port-au-Prince where he was greeted at the airport by thousands of "Lavalas." The following day he was arrested. An army officer held a pistol at Aristide's temple and was about to squeeze the trigger when a sergeant jerked his hand.

"They should have killed the son-of-a-bitch right there," a wealthy businessman said.

Aristide spent his exile first in Venezuela and then in the United States, working to develop international support. The United Nations backed a trade embargo, intended to get the coup leaders to step down. Rather, it was a strong blow to Haiti's weak economy. Besides, the coup regime was supported by massive profits from the drug trade, thanks to the Haitian army's affiliation with the Cali Cartel.

A massive pro-Aristide demonstration by Haitian expats in New York City, with crowds estimated at 250,000, urged U.S. President Bill Clinton to deliver on his election promise to return Aristide to Haiti. International pressure, the U.N. and the U.S. persuaded the military regime to back down, and Clinton deployed U.S. troops.

On Oct. 15, 1994, the Clinton administration returned Aristide to Haiti to complete his term in office.

In February 1996, Rene Preval was sworn in as the 41st president of Haiti, the first smooth transition from one president to another. Aristide formed a new political party, Famni Lavalas, to "get closer" to the people.

Four years later, Aristide was back in office, winning with 92 percent of the vote, although the turnout was a less than enthusiastic 50 percent of the voters.

In February 2004, the assassination of gang leader Amiot Metayer sparked a violent rebellion that culminated in Aristide's removal from office. Insurgents took control of the North and eventually invaded the capital. Guy Philippe, who stormed the presidential palace in a failed 2001 coup, and his rebel forces surrounded Port-au-Prince and announced plans to arrest Aristide.

Under disputed circumstances, Aristide resigned and was flown out of the country on a U.S. military plane with assistance from Canada and France on Feb. 28, 2004. Aristide claimed he was "kidnapped." He was first brought to the Central African Republic and then to South Africa. He was told he had to leave Haiti immediately or he would be killed and "a lot of Haitians would be killed."

Aristide and his family lived in a government villa in Pretoria, was provided staff and received a salary from South Africa. He became an honorary research fellow at the University of South Africa, learned Zulu, and in 2007 received a doctorate in African languages.

On Jan. 12, 2010, Aristide sent condolences to victims of the earthquake just a few hours after it occurred, telling them he wanted to return to help rebuild the country. But he added he was not allowed to leave South Africa.

He did depart from his exile the following year and upon arriving at the Port-au-Prince airport he was greeted by thousands of supporters.

"Today may the Haitian people end exiles and *coups d'etat* while peacefully moving from social exclusion to inclusion," he told the crowd.

Amnesty International said that after Aristide's departure in 2004, Haiti was "descending into a severe humanitarian and human rights crisis."

In 2012, Aristide was still the champion of the poor, and had the biggest base of any political figure in the country. He was considered the only really popular, democratically elected leader that Haiti had ever had.

Aristide was born into poverty in Port-Salut in 1953. His father died when he was a toddler and he and his mother moved to Port-au-Prince. He started school with the priests of the Salesian order, and graduated from College Notre Dame in Cap Haitien before entering the priesthood. After completing post-graduate studies, he traveled to Europe before returning to Haiti for his ordination as a Salesian priest.

During the first three decades of Aristide's life, Haiti was ruled by the family dictatorships of Francois "Papa Doc" Duvalier and his son Jean-Claude "Baby Doc" Duvalier. The misery endured by Haiti's poor affected him, and Aristide became an outspoken critic of "Duvalierism."

He was an exponent of liberation theology. He often denounced the regime, and his criticism didn't go unnoticed. The provincial delegate of the Salesian Order, under pressure, sent Aristide to three years exile in Montreal, Canada.

Aristide was a leading figure in the *"ti legliz"* movement, Creole for "little church." He founded an orphanage for street children, and he became a voice for the aspirations of Haiti's dispossessed.

He survived at least four assassination attempts. The St. John Bosco massacre occurred on Sept. 11, 1988, when more than 100 armed *Toutons Macoute* wearing red arm bands forced their way into St. John Bosco Church as Aristide began Sunday Mass.

As army troops and police stood by, the men fired machine guns at the congregation and attacked fleeing parishioners with machetes. Aristides's church was burned to the ground. Thirteen people were killed, and 77 were wounded. Aristide survived and went into hiding.

Salesian officials ordered Aristide to leave Haiti, but tens of thousands protested, blocking his access to the airport. In December 1988, Aristide was expelled from the Salesians. The order said the priest's political activities and "incitement to hatred and violence" was out of line with his role as a clergyman.

Aristide appealed the decision: "The crime of which I stand accused is the crime of preaching food for all men and women." He later added, "The solution is revolution, first in the spirit of the Gospel. Jesus could not accept people going hungry."

In 1994, Aristide left the priesthood, ending years of tension with the church over his criticism of its hierarchy and his espousal of liberation theology. Two years later he married Mildred Trouillot, an attorney, who was born in the Bronx. They met at an Aristide lecture, and she went to work for Aristide's "government in exile" in Washington, D.C.

Resources:

Peter A. Geniesse, The Post-Crescent, Appleton, Wis.; 'A human rights nightmare'; Jan. 31, 1993

Wikipedia, the Free Encyclopedia; "Jean-Bertrand Aristide'; June 21, 2015.

CNN Gant Daily; 'Jean-Bertrand Aristide Fast Facts'; June 18, 2015.

CHAPTER SEVENTEEN

Photo by Peter A. Geniesse

A young boy stands alongside a sewage ditch amid the squalor of Cite Soleil, Haiti, among the worst slums in the hemisphere. Father Lawrence Bohnen, a Salesian missionary from Holland, known as the "Saint of Soleil," established schools and fed thousands over the course of more than four decades.

"It's now 1779 in Haiti. I hope there will be a revolution. But It would be better if it were peaceful."
–Lawrence Bohnen

CHAPTER SEVENTEEN

FATHER 'BEANS' BOHNEN

1915—1996
Port-au-Prince, Haiti   1993

They called him "Father Beans," this Salesian missionary from Holland who came to Haiti back in 1954 after his order was expelled from Hanoi. He was a teacher of Latin and Greek in Vietnam until the communist Viet Minh defeated the French.

He was sent to teach in the slums of Port-au-Prince. But there was no market for the classics. Few could write their names. Most were malnourished. All were oppressed by an endless series of dictators and military regimes.

So he started a cluster of one-room schools and found some teachers who knew a bit more than their pupils. Then he established a soup kitchen. Beans was the noon meal. Beans and rice. For many, it was their only meal of the day.

That was more than a half-century ago.

In 1993 Bohnen was overseeing more than 180 schools that teach and feed 25,000 students a day in Cite Soleil. He was in his 80s, recovering from prostate and colon cancer operations, but he was determined to stick around to see another generation of Haitians rise up from their surroundings.

And they were dire, indeed.

More than 200,000 people lived in cardboard and scrap metal shacks the size of packing crates, most without water or electricity, on a dismal plain near Port-au-Prince's waterfront.

Mountains of smoldering garbage clouded the skies. Fetid open sewers crisscrossed the settlements, called "Boston" and "Brooklyn." There's a rotting plank which spans a ditch oozing with industrial and human waste. Bohnen calls it his "Brooklyn Bridge." It led to one of his mini-schools.

Bohnen has never gotten used to the stench. Nor the hopelessness that breeds in Cite Soleil, the "City of Sun."

"Nobody should be living here," he said. "This is against human dignity."

Cite Soleil is located on the western end of the runway of Toussaint Louverture International Airport, and adjoins the former Hasco Haitian American sugar complex. It started as a benign residential area for 52 families in 1958.

It soon became a dumping ground for people and refuse.

A series of mysterious fires in other slum sectors forced thousands of people to move into areas unprepared for habitation. The government encouraged squatters from the countryside to settle there even though it lacked such basic services as sewers, water, electricity and streets.

Half of the houses in Cite Soleil were made of cement with a metal roof and half were made completely with scavenged materials. Sixty percent of the houses had no access to a latrine.

Within two decades, Cite Soleil had the dubious distinction of being one of the biggest slums in the hemisphere. It also was the poorest and the most dangerous.

For years the area was ruled by gangs, each controlling their own sectors. They roamed the streets, terrorizing the neighborhoods. There were more than 30 armed factions controlling access in Cite Soleil. After the devastating 2010 earthquake, it took nearly two weeks for relief aid to arrive in Cite Soleil.

In 2007, the United Nations Stabilization Mission, an international team of military and police sent to Haiti on a peace-keeping mission in 2004, focused its attention on Cite Soleil, attempting to curb the power of the gangs.

The UN team included 8,940 military personnel and 3,711 police, mostly from Brazil and Latin American countries. Their UN Security Council mandate was effective until October 2010.

In early February of 2007, some 700 UN troops flooded Cite Soleil, resulting in a major gun battle. It took three months and 800 arrests to lessen the power of the gangs.

Though the gangs no longer rule, murder, rape, kidnaping, looting and shootings are still common.

The area has been called "a microcosm of all the ills in Haitian society," everything from endemic unemployment, illiteracy, non-existent public services, and unsanitary conditions, to rampant crime and armed violence.

Father Bohnen's hope for Haiti's future was riding on Jean-Bertrand Aristide's shoulders. They were close friends. He taught him in his mini-schools, and they were both Salesian priests, a generation apart.

In 1993, with Aristide was still in forced exile in the U.S., Bohnen was singing his praises. "When Aristide gets back in power, the country will be back on track," he said. "It won't be easy to rebuild Haiti, but Aristide will do it."

He likened his former pupil and fellow Salesian to Martin Luther King Jr. The slain American civil rights leader was a dreamer and so was Aristide, he said.

"You can kill the dreamer, but you can't kill the dream," he added, noting that Aristide had survived several assassination attempts.

Bohnen was an unflinching supporter of Aristide, bucking the sentiments of most Haitian bishops and many in his own religious order. Aristide left the Salesians after a rule was invoked barring members from politics. He also bowed out of the priesthood under pressure from the Vatican.

But that didn't deter Bohnen's enthusiasm for his most-famous alumnus. Even while gangs of *attaches* roamed Cite Soleil, ruthlessly ridding it of all mention of the exiled president, Bohnen maintained a large banner over one mini-school that said, "Father Aristide, Old Grad."

Bohnen was invited to the presidential palace and Aristide visited his colleague in Cite Soleil. But the Dutch priest shunned the spotlight. He'd rather focus on the future of his schools.

Countless slum dwellers learned to read and write. Many made it through junior high and technical schools, and at least 12,000 had learned a trade. Each year 1,000 students were able to escape Cite Soleil. Their places were quickly taken up by those migrating from the barren countryside.

He figured his sites had served more than 70 million meals by 1993. "It's the biggest diner's club in the world," he said. Much of the food came free from the European Union.

Once his warehouse was looted, and his longtime friend, Dutch Consul Rob J. Padberg quickly secured replacement commodities. It was the first time in 40 years that the food distribution system had been halted.

"But feeding is not the fundamental solution," he said. "Education is."

Bohnen started his Haitian ministry in 1954 in La Saline, Port-au-Prince's slum of the day. He was sent to establish a trade school, but he soon discovered that most of his prospective students were illiterate. So he opened a couple of elementary schools in shacks.

Later he moved to nearby Cite Rouge and set up a similar school system. But the government, determined to get rid of the eyesore at the expense of the people, burned down the squatter settlement. Bohnen and the poor then moved to Cite Soleil.

In the early years, his centers educated about 3,000 a year. By 1993, the 183 mini-schools affected more than 10 times that number each day. Bohnen provided the teachers and the food, but each community had to provide the one-room school.

"The rules of the system say it's the promotion of the personal initiative of the poor people themselves," he said. "When we've helped 25,000 pupils, we've helped 50,000 parents too."

The best pupils are accepted into the five central middle schools. From there they can feed into a junior high school and then to the technical school he was sent to start 40 years ago. Each year about 200 boys and 150 girls graduate from that two-year job-training program.

Bohnen – which means "beans" in Dutch – frequently traveled to the U.S., Canada and Europe to raise funds for his school system. He needed to raise $1.5 million a year to cover his annual expenses.

He recruited two other Salesian priests, one a Belgian and the other a Haitian, to take his place once he decided to retire.

And he's excited about the prospects of a new, four-year teachers' college that was established by his team in Cite Soleil. That meant his 900 instructors would be "more than a chapter ahead of their students," he said. And that meant that more students would go on to technical schools and some would make it to the universities.

"Someday," he said, "Maybe Cite Soleil won't be such a slum."

Bohnen long was an outspoken critic of Haiti's ruling elite. "After two centuries of independence, this is what they get –two centuries of government by a small minority."

He likened the setting to that of the eve of the French Revolution. "It's 1779 in Haiti," he said. "I hope there will be a revolution. But it would be better if it were peaceful."

Although the feared *Tontons Macoute* and right-wing government thugs, called *attaches,* often raided and burned suspected Artistide strongholds in Cite Soleil, slaughtering scores of slum dwellers, Bohnen rarely had been threatened and had never been arrested by the military.

"They were in no hurry to take over my business," he said.

Resources:

Peter A. Geniesse; The Post-Crescent, Appleton, Wis.; 'Learning, teaching the hard way'; Feb. 1, 1993.

National Catholic Reporter; "Father Beans' educates in Haitian slum"; Jan. 20, 1995.

Wikipedia, the free encyclopedia; "Cite Soleil" and "UN Mission in Haiti"; June 23, 2015.

Chapter Eighteen

Photos by Peter A. Geniesse

Lavaud Cheristin, right, and Evans Orelien attended college together in Wisconsin and returned to Haiti to establish private schools in their hometowns of Hinche and Pont Sonde in the 1990s.

"Our Doc, who art in the National Palace for life, hallowed be Thy name. . .Give us this day our new Haiti and never forgive the trespasses of the anti-patriots."
–Francois "Papa Doc" Duvalier

CHAPTER EIGHTEEN

LAVAUD CHERISTIN, EVANS ORELIEN

Hinche and Pont Sonde, Haiti   1995

Lavaud Cheristin, 30, recalled hearing his folks talk of brighter days. They belonged to his grandfather, who raised corn and vegetables, bananas and mangoes, chickens and pigs and lots of children on a farm not far from the Central Plateau capital of Hinche.

Both of his grandparents lived to be more than 100, in a land where the life expectancy now is 56

"Yes," said Cheristin. "Their lives were much better than ours."

Evans Orelien, 31, agreed. His father's family once owned acres of rich agricultural land near St. Marc on the edge of the Artibonite Valley, the country's rice bowl.

But that was a couple of generations ago. That was before the land was parceled into tiny plots by large families, before the government, the military and the wealthy teamed up to confiscate farms, before drought and a desperate people rendered the land infertile and turned trees into charcoal, setting off an ecological crisis throughout the countryside.

Vast forests once covered 75 percent of Haiti. Today less than 7 per cent is treed. Only 10 percent is arable, although 43 percent, largely eroded and saline, remains under cultivation.

Cheristin and Orelien, too, remember better times. Even during the Duvalier dictatorships, their families had enough food. But then came successive military regimes where oppression was all that the people got from their government.

The worldwide economic embargo, aimed to oust the leaders who sent President Jean-Bertrand Aristide into exile in 1991, placed the poor on the brink of starvation.

The two knew all too well how the other half lived. They had shared an apartment in Appleton, Wis., during their two years of studies at Fox Valley Technical College. They got to like Big Macs and Saturday afternoons at the Fox River Mall. They had friends who had big houses with pools, and sports cars in their garages. They were free to visit Door County and Chicago and other parts of the U.S.

Then they returned to their hometowns in Haiti where they lived in hovels without electricity or running water – or freedom.

One of their fellow Haitian students in the Third World program sponsored by the U.S. Agency for International Development opted for New York, preferring illegal status to returning to Haiti.

But Cheristin and Orelien had to return. They had started schools for the poor in their villages before they left for the United States., and had plans to offer technical training to give their students a better chance for jobs and a bit brighter future.

Both were buoyed by the promise of Jean-Bertrand Aristide, but one month after they arrived in Haiti, the president was overthrown by a military coup. Their schools were shut down and their teachers were targeted.

One night in Port-au-Prince, Orelien was attacked by a pack of thugs who pressed a pistol to his temple while pinning him to the pavement. The gun didn't go off.

Political violence racked the capital in the wake of the coup. Aristide supporters were targeted by former members of the *Tontons Macoute*. Every morning there were bodies on the streets, with placards of warnings on their chests. Pedestrians walked swiftly around the corpses in downtown Port-au-Prince, fearing that if they paused, they could be next.

The *Tontons Macoute*, goons who formed the private army of the Duvalier's dictatorships for generations, had established an insidious spy system where neighbors were rewarded for turning in neighbors.

All gatherings were suspect. A meeting of school teachers in a private home called for trusted monitors at all entrances to stave off spies.

Orelien spent several months in Florida with relatives during the bloody military regime, but he was determined to return to Pont-Sonde and his College Notre Dame. Cheristin stayed in Hinche, keeping a low profile at Centre Oswald Duran, his school without walls.

Both men had college degrees. Both spoke four languages – Creole, French, Spanish and English. Both could have landed good jobs, either in Port-au-Prince or in the U.S.

But each realized that he represented hope in their hometowns.

For generations of Haitians, hope has become a rare commodity.

Haiti once was called the Pearl of the Antilles, the single richest colony in the world. That was back in the 18th century when 40,000 Frenchmen ruled 700,000 slaves from West Africa.

In 1803, a slave revolt, led by Toussaint L'Ouverture, defeated a force of 28,000 troops sent by Napoleon Bonaparte. The following year, Haiti became the first free black republic and the second independent country in the hemisphere, after the United States.

It was a lush tropical land with sugar cane plantations and mountains blanketed with thick mahogany forests. But as the population exploded, its landscape took a heavy toll. Trees were cut down to be used for charcoal fuel. Hungry peasants stripped the land to plant food.

Today, brown mountains, scarred by erosion, stand in stark contrast to the highland forests of neighboring Dominican Republic.

Political instability didn't help matters. The country was ruled by 22 dictators who took office by way of political coups in the 19th century. Then came the U.S. Marines who administered Haiti from 1915 to 1934, leading to the Duvalier regimes.

In 1957, a country doctor, who had gained fame in the eradication of yaws, became president. Francois "Papa Doc" Duvalier, fearing a future military coup, established his own protective goon squad, the *Tontons Macoute*, setting off a reign of terror that lasted 29 years.

Thousands were killed by the *Tontons Macoute*, and Duvalier's power was bolstered by his promotion of voodoo, the tribal African religion. He declared himself president for life, and became a deity figure.

"Our Doc, who art in the National Palace for life, hallowed be Thy name by present and future generations," he wrote. "Thy will be done in Port-au-Prince and in the provinces. Give us this day our new Haiti and never forgive the trespasses of the anti-patriots."

Before he died in 1971, he arranged for his 19-year-old son, Jean-Claude, to succeed him. "Baby Doc" continued his father's ruthless rule until he was overthrown by the military in 1986.

"Baby Doc" fled with his family to France with $800 million from the Haitian treasury, more than four times the country's annual revenues.

The poor danced in the streets and took revenge on the *Tontons Macoute*, using machetes and the "flaming necklace" to gruesomely kill them.

Again there was political chaos. In the next four years, there were five more military coups.

When Aristide was elected with 67 percent of the vote in December 1990, it marked the nearly 200-year-old nation's first free elections.

"Now things will change," Cheristin said at the time, comparing Aristide to Haiti's revolutionary war hero Francois Toussaint L'Ouverture who led the slave revolt against the French in 1803.

But one month later, Aristide was gone, ousted by the military. Dreams were dashed. There were no jobs. Hope was lost.

Lavaud and Evans were counting on a partnership with the new government to establish technical schools to train people for jobs in their communities. Political chaos, once again, had put progress on hold.

Both Lavaud and Evans started their own schools in 1986 soon after getting their "philosophy" degrees from high school. They rented tiny buildings, promised teachers $100 a month to instruct three or more shifts a day and soon more than 200 pupils were paying $1 a month to learn the basics.

There were more private than public schools in Haiti; both charged tuition, both required uniforms. About half of the school age children attended classes. For the others, there was no money and no room.

In most schools, classes of 50 or more were common. Few provided text books. The students learned by rote, meticulously writing down everything the teacher chalked on the board.

Few schools had electricity. Fewer had indoor plumbing. Many of the classes were conducted outdoors on benches, with chalkboards tacked onto the outside walls.

Evans' school, College Notre Dame, was located in Pont-Sonde, a village of 50,000 near St. Marc on the coast. In 1986 he started classes in the former *Tontons Macoute* headquarters shortly after Baby Doc was ousted. Later he moved his school into a cluster of rundown wood and concrete buildings where 375 students packed four tiny classrooms in three shifts.

Lavaud's school, Centre Oswald Durand, was located in Hinche, an isolated mountain village of 40,000 about 70 miles – and eight hours by 4-wheel drive – from Port-au-Prince. There were multiple shifts to educate 350 students, from pre-school to high school.

Both Lavaud and Evans received some financial support from schools and churches they visited in Wisconsin's Fox Valley. But most of the time, it didn't pay the bills.

In 1995, four months after Aristide returned to Haiti, Lavaud broke ground for a six-classroom school on the outskirts of Hinche. Someday, he said, there'd be a second floor and maybe even a third devoted to a new technical school.

Before the building could open, however, there was another coup, and a new set of dictators who cared little about the future of education in Haiti. Once again their plans for technical schools were put on hold.

Evans had more financial concerns. He got no help from the government, he couldn't pay the teachers, and they walked off the job.

He also faced physical threats. His parents, who had lived in Miami for years, suggested Evans and his wife move there.

Millions of Haitians, including 80 percent of its college graduates, have left the country and have settled abroad, sending remittances to their families that total more than 50 percent of Haiti's gross domestic product.

It's estimated that 800,000 live in neighboring Dominican Republic and at least 600,000 live in the U.S. Another 100,000 live in Canada, mostly in French-speaking Quebec.

Lavaud, with help from mission support in the U.S., has weathered Haiti's political storms, and after nearly 30 years is nearing his goal of providing education and technical training to the needy in his hometown.

"I just couldn't have done this if God hadn't called me to do it," the now ordained minister said.

Haiti has been in the eye of the storm forever. Its position in the Caribbean assures that hurricanes and tropical storms are frequent visitors. But its eroded slopes, and treeless valleys flirt with disaster each time heavy rains fall.

Other Caribbean nations get hit with the same storms, but most are prepared for them. Haiti's poor-- and most are desperately poor – are unable to escape their dilapidated housing for higher ground, and many drown.

In 2004, Tropical Storm Jeanne skimmed the north coast of Haiti, leaving more than 3,000 dead, due to floods and landslides, mostly in the city of Gonaives. In 2008, Haiti was pummeled by four tropical storms and hurricanes within two months, leaving more than 800 dead and 800,000 in need of humanitarian aid.

Then there was the earthquake!

On the evening of Jan. 12, 2010, Haiti was struck with a magnitude 7.0 earthquake, the country's most severe earthquake in 200 years.

Port-au-Prince, just 16 miles from the epicenter, suffered catastrophic damage and loss of life.

Initial reports, which had the death toll listed at 316,000 people, was later scaled down to about 100,000. More than 1,500,000 people, 16 percent of the nation's population of 9.3 million, were left homeless.

Among those who died in the earthquake was the Catholic archbishop of Port-au-Prince, Joseph Serge Miot. At least 85 United Nations personnel died when their headquarters collapsed. About 200 guests at the upscale Hotel Montana in Port-au-Prince died when the structure was destroyed. Thirty members of the Haitian national soccer team were listed among the casualties.

Some 250,000 residences and 30,000 commercial and public buildings collapsed or were severely damaged. These included the Presidential Palace, the National Assembly building and the Port-au-Prince Cathedral. The Prison Civile was destroyed, allowing 4,000 to escape.

Haiti's educational system collapsed. Half of the nation's schools and the three main universities in Port-au-Prince were affected. More than 1,300 schools and 50 health care facilities were destroyed.

Centre Oswald Durand, Lavaud Cheristan's new school in Hinche, 70 miles from the quake's epicenter, escaped damage.

The severity of the 7.0 earthquake was further amplified by more than 50 after-shocks. The lack of building codes, poor housing conditions and ineffective government combined to turn an often-manageable quake elsewhere into a national tragedy.

The world responded. Within two days of the earthquake, more than 20 countries, led by the U.S., Canada and the Dominican Republic, had sent military personnel on rescue operations. The supercarrier USS Carl Vinson arrived Jan. 15 with 600,000 emergency food rations, 100,000 ten-liter water containers and 19 helicopters to deliver the items to impassible regions.

While thousands of Good Samaritans and millions of pledged dollars poured into Haiti in the wake of the quake, the magnitude of the disaster stalled the nation's recovery two years later. Some 500,000 were still living in tents in 2012.

Still, there's an element of hope.

It's found in a community called Canaan, named for the biblical promise of promise and prosperity. Before the earthquake, it was a dusty wasteland just a dozen miles from the northern edge of Port-au-Prince.

In 2015, some 250,000 settlers, many with money sent from relatives living abroad, have begun a new life in new homes. It's a $100 million project. It even has the support of the Haitian government, which is working on a master plan to install basic services in Canaan.

With $14 million from the American Red Cross and USAID, the pilot project calls for paved roads, schools, water and electricity, along with assuring that new houses meet construction standards and building codes.

The biggest fear is that Canaan might become another slum like Cite Soleil. However, since the homesteaders are putting their own money and sweat into the settlement, Haitian officials believe they will be more open to urban planning to protect their investments.

"We'll see if the government is really serious about helping us here," said one new small businessman.

Resources:

Associated Press: 'Haiti tries urban planning'; June 26, 2015.

Paul Farmer: 'Haiti after the Earthquake'; Public Affairs, 2011.

Peter A. Geniesse: 'Technical schools a dream on hold'; The Post-Crescent, Appleton, WI, Feb. 2, 1993.

Wikipedia, the free encyclopedia: 'Haiti' and '2010 Haiti Earthquake', Oct. 2. 2013.

CHAPTER NINETEEN

Photo by Peter A. Geniesse

Bishop Samuel Ruiz gathered in solidarity with fellow Latin American bishops at the cathedral in San Cristóbol de las Casas in January 1994 as the Mexican military cracked down on the indigenous militants.

"It's sad that he had to take up the same cause five centuries later."
– of Samuel Ruiz

CHAPTER NINETEEN

'RED' BISHOP SAMUEL RUIZ

1925-2011
San Cristóbal de Las Casas, Mexico   1994

It was New Year's Day, 1994, when the cultures collided.

It was the birthday of the North American Free Trade Agreement, the much-heralded scheme aimed to bring Mexico's citizens and economy into the 21st century.

The milestone was greeted by massive protests in Chiapas, the nation's poorest and most indigenous state, on the Guatemalan frontier.

The Zapatistas, rag-tag insurgents under the leadership of a masked man called Subcomandante Marcos, seized four villages and the city of San Cristóbal de las Casas. They sought a public platform to tell the world that Mexico was embarking on a plan that would spell disaster for the Indians and the poor throughout Mexico.

They feared losing control of their lands. They opposed the neo-liberal globalization policies. They believed that would destroy their peasant way of life.

Mexico sent in its troops the following day, and numerous clashes left at least 65 dead.

Ten days later, a ceasefire was brokered by Catholic Bishop Samuel Ruiz, of the Diocese of San Cristóbal. However, the conflict flared and simmered amid attempts at negotiations over the next decade.

The Zapatista National Liberation Army is named after Emiliano Zapata, the popular hero of the 1910-1917 Mexican revolution, who defended poor peasants' right to free land seized from wealthy landowners.

At least one-third of the population of Chiapas is considered indigenous. Throughout Mexico, there are more than 20 million Indians. Some, like the Lacandón, are direct descendants of the Maya, and have been living in Chiapas much like their ancestors did for the past 500 years. Most live off the land and tend small parcels for growing corn and beans.

Under NAFTA, they feared, their land and their livelihoods would be jeopardized. Crop subsidies would be curtailed, and the peasant farmers would be forced to compete in the marketplace with imported U.S. products which were artificially fertilized, mechanically harvested and genetically modified.

They had good reason to fear for their land and their future. President Carlos Salinas, in preparation for NAFTA, already had repealed existing agrarian reform legislation in 1992. He allowed communal *ejido* lands to be sold off, rented, or to be dissolved entirely. Land distribution programs were to be discontinued and small farmers were to lose access to credit and state price supports.

The Zapatistas continued to issue warnings, and gathered sympathy throughout Mexico but they could not derail the North American Free Trade Agreement.

They called him "Tatik," or father in the Tzotzil Indian language. He was their defender, their pastor, their champion, their friend.

For more than 40 years, Bishop Samuel Ruiz García was more Mayan than Mexican. He had inherited the diocese of San Cristóbal de las Casas from the Spanish priest who fought to defend the rights of the Indians in the face of the *Conquistadores* some 500 years earlier. He saw it as his legacy.

San Cristóbal is named for Fray Bartolomé de las Casas, the 16th century Dominican missionary who became the first bishop of Chiapas in 1542. Fray Bartolomé, whose wealthy family was associated with Christopher Columbus, decried the horrors of the conquest and the colonization of the New World.

He lobbied the Spanish monarchy for laws to end the corrupt *encomienda* system which legalized slavery. He received death threats from the colonists for his efforts.

Five centuries later, Bishop Ruiz took up the cause. And he received the same treatment.

Not long after arriving in San Cristóbal in 1959, Ruiz set out on a mule tour of his diocese, visiting every town and village in his jurisdiction. He was stunned by the poverty and marginalization of the indigenous communities of Chiapas.

Ruiz gradually underwent a series of conversion experiences, leading him to take up the cause of the Mayan people in his diocese, as well as developing an "inculturated" approach to indigenous evangelization.

His social conscious was awakened during the Second Vatican Council. The Catholic Church was being urged to be more involved in their communities in eradicating social problems, especially in Central and South America. The vernacular was introduced, replacing Latin as the language of liturgy.

It inspired Ruiz to translate the scripture into local indigenous languages – he spoke four-- which led to a renewed emphasis on inculturation.

Vatican II also called for bringing the Catholic faith to people in a way that reflected their own cultures.

Ruiz served leading roles at the Latin American bishops' conference at Medellin, Colombia, in 1968, which declared the church's preferential option for the poor. He also became an advocate of liberation theology and Base Communities, abandoning the traditional approach of Europeanizing indigenous peoples.

Catechists began fostering discussion of economic and political matters that impacted people's daily lives. The indigenous poor no longer had to silently accept the low wages they earned on plantations, the lack of security in their land titles, the corruption of government agencies and the abuses of merchants and landowners.

Ruiz also tried to fend off the rapid growth of Protestant denominations by adapting to Indian customs. He relied heavily on married male lay workers because Indian culture granted more respect to men who had children than to celibate men like priests.

He trained Indian catechists to organize village assemblies throughout the mountains and jungles of his diocese. By the end of his tenure in 2000, there were more than 20,000 catechists in Chiapas.

The Zapatista uprising had been simmering in the mountains and the jungles ever since a dozen college-educated young Mexicans, headed by a masked man soon to be known only as "Subcomandante Marcos," came to San Cristóbal in 1983. He was deemed to be the new Che Guevara, fighting for the rights of the indigenous people.

"We didn't go to war to kill or be killed," Marcos said. "We went to war in order to be heard."

His message was picked up by a wide variety of solidarity groups, in Mexico and throughout the world. It was even amplified by the U.S. rock group, "Rage against the Machine," which dedicated several pieces to the cause.

As a young man, Marcos was politically radicalized by the Tlatelolco massacre in Mexico City, where the military killed several hundred students who were demonstrating against the government 10 days before the opening of the 1968 Summer Olympics.

President Gustavo Diaz Ordaz ordered the army to occupy the National Autonomous University of Mexico, the nation's largest. It was the first time a Latin American country had hosted the Olympics and Diaz didn't want the rebellious students to upstage the event.

On Oct. 2, about 10,000 students gathered in the *Plaza de Tres Culturas* to protest the government action. They were soon surrounded by 5,000 soldiers, 200 tanks and trucks, with helicopters hovering over the plaza.

Before the night was over, perhaps as many as 300 were dead from gunshot wounds and thousands more were injured and/or arrested. The Mexican government, facing one of its worst crises ever, launched a huge cover-up operation. It took 40 years for the truth to come out.

Among the facts revealed was that the U.S. had a role in the massacre. The CIA, fearing the riots would disrupt the Olympic Games, had been monitoring student actions each day. The U.S. sent military radios, weapons and ammunition, along with riot control training materials to Mexico before and during the crisis.

It wasn't the first time the U.S. had intervened in the domestic affairs of a sovereign Latin American nation. And it wouldn't be the last.

A quarter century later, on New Year's Day 1994, another insurrection delivered a message across the country from its southernmost state, Chiapas. It was the day NAFTA went into effect, and Mexico's indigenous had been left out of the process.

They had lost communal lands when the *ejidos* were sacrificed to prepare for NAFTA. They feared free trade would put an end to their way of life.

The Zapatista Army of National Liberation, or EZLN, a loosely formed coalition of Mayan Indians numbering about 3,000, took control of four Chiapas municipalities. They were led by a masked man, a poet who claimed to be a graduate of the Sorbonne University in Paris, with a *nom de guerre* of Subcomandante Marcos, a name he borrowed from a friend who was killed at an army roadblock.

His real name surfaced much later as Rafael Sebastian Guillen Vincente, a native of Tampico who moved to Mexico City, graduated from the National Autonomous University of Mexico and joined the Forces of National Liberation, the predecessor of EZLN.

The Zapatistas wanted to send a message to Mexico City.

The government wasn't interested in their message. It was having a peso crisis, and it didn't need an indigenous distraction on the birthday of NAFTA, heralded to transform Mexico into a First World nation.

Besides, it had gotten a message from Chase Manhattan Bank in New York "to get rid of the Zapatistas" in exchange for full bailout financing, promised by U.S. President Bill Clinton.

The next day, thousands of troops were sent to Chiapas to crush the uprising, and over the course of the next 10 days, 145 people were dead and hundreds were arrested.

On Jan. 15, my wife Jill and I interrupted our vacation in Huatulco and hopped a bus to San Cristóbal to see for ourselves what was taking place in our favorite colonial city.

We checked in at Na Bolom, a 19th century hacienda that doubles as a museum and an occasional haven for indigenous on the run. It was hosted by famed archaeologist Frans Bloom and his ethnologist wife Gertrude, who had spent much of their lives studying and befriending the Lacandón, the most primitive of the Mayan Indians.

Two of the Lacandón leaders, wanted by the Mexican military, had taken refuge at Na Bolom. Through a translator, we learned that paramilitaries had targeted "Tatik," their Tzotzil name for Bishop Ruiz. In the past, he had received numerous death threats from the coffee and cattle barons who ruled much of Chiapas.

This time, they said, Tatik's life was in real danger. That evening there was to be a special Mass in the Cathedral, and they feared he would be assassinated at the altar. As a journalist, it was my duty to attend.

The plaza around the church was a war zone with hundreds of soldiers, armed with automatic weapons, taking up positions as Bishop Ruiz arrived with his contingent of 100 Mayan bodyguards. They processed into the church and surrounded the sanctuary, filled with priests and a half-dozen bishops from throughout Latin America.

With all those solidarity witnesses, there would be no assassination that night. In November 1997, however, he was ambushed by gunmen on a mountain road but he escaped without injury.

They called him the "Red" bishop, those racist foes who labeled Ruiz as communist for his support of the Mayan's simple demands of "work, land, housing, food, health, education, independence, freedom, justice and peace."

In 1989, Bishop Ruiz founded the Fray Bartolomé de Las Casas Rights Center to push back against increasing violence against indigenous and campesino activists in his diocese. He cast light on abuses suffered by Indians and sought to bring them into the church as equals with other Mexicans, challenging the rigidly stratified social order.

Bishop Ruiz's Mayan sympathies earned him enemies among the landed class in Chiapas and the Indians who opposed the rebels. He supported the Zapatistas' goal of fighting injustice, but he did not endorse their violent tactics.

His advocacy and egalitarian views brought him into conflict with the Mexican government, which accused him of fomenting the violent uprising in Chiapas in 1994.

He also rankled the Vatican, which said he had strayed from ecclesiastical principles to create a politicized ethnic church, and in 1993 he was publicly invited to step down. The following year Pope John Paul II named conservative Bishop Raul Vera López as diocesan coadjutor to keep an eye on Bishop Ruiz.

Mexican clerics rallied to his defense, however, and he remained as bishop until 2000. Obeying Vatican rules, Ruiz retired when he turned 75. Two years later the Vatican ordered a halt to a program Ruiz had initiated that had ordained more than 300 married Indian deacons.

For four years, Bishop Ruiz mediated peace talks between the government and the Zapatistas. Accords were signed in February, 1995, in the Chiapas village of San Andrés Larráinzar. They called for recognition of the indigenous culture and its right to land and autonomy.

President Ernesto Zedillo signed the document but he soon reneged over the accord's implications. He accused Ruiz of favoring the rebels and preaching a "theology of violence."

Social tensions, armed conflict and para-military incidents increased as the peace talks floundered. On Dec. 22, 1997, government-backed para-militaries murdered 45 civilians, including 21 women and 15 children, in the remote village of Acteal. The massacre of the Tzotzil villagers, who were attending a church service, was tied to Mexico's ruling party. The fallout led to the end of the PRI's 71-year reign over the nation's politics.

The massacre also had international implications as the European Commission, which was negotiating a free trade agreement with Mexico, condemned the para-military violence and urged President Zedillo to re-initiate the peace process.

PAN President Vincente Fox, who campaigned on a promise to solve the conflict with the Zapatistas "within 15 minutes," took office in November 2000, pledging to honor the San Andrés accords.

To build support for the accords, the Zapatistas mounted a 16-day caravan, bringing Marcos and other EZLN *comandantes* to Mexico City in February and March 2001. A crowd estimated at 250,000 filled the Zócolo in solidarity with the Zapatistas' demands.

Nevertheless, Congress gutted the accords and the Zapatistas returned to Chiapas empty-handed.

In 1998, Bishop Ruiz resigned as peace mediator and his committee disbanded. He accused the government of "simulating" a peace process. "There can be no peace if there is no justice," he said. Ruiz continued to advocate for human rights for the indigenous until his death in 2011.

Ruiz was nominated for the Nobel Peace Prize for three straight years in the mid-1990s by such notables as Rigoberta Menchú and Adolfo Pérez Esquivel. Among other awards, he received the Simon Bolivar International Prize by UNESCO in 2000 for his work defending the indigenous peoples of Chiapas.

Upon his death, Mexican President Felipe Calderon said, "Samuel Ruiz struggled to build a more just, more equal, dignified Mexico without discrimination," adding "he always acted with integrity and moral rectitude.

"His death represents a great loss for Mexico," he said.

Mexican writer Homero Aridjis called "Don Samuel" one of the "great consciences" of human rights. He praised him for following in the footsteps of Fray Bartolomé de Las Casas.

"It's sad that he had to take up the same cause five centuries later," Aridjis said.

Resources:

Peter A. Geniesse: "Illegal: NAFTA refugees forced to flee;" iUniverse, Bloomington, IN, 2010.

Julia Preston: New York Times; "Defender of Mexico's Mayans," Jan. 26, 2011.

Sergio Muñoz: Los Angeles Times; "Samuel Ruiz," May 10, 1998.

Manuel de la Cruz: Associated Press; "Pro-Indian Mexican Bishop Dead at 86," Jan. 24, 2011.

Wikipedia, the free encyclopedia: "Chiapas conflict," "Samuel Ruiz," and "Sub. Marcos," July 9, 2015.

CHAPTER TWENTY

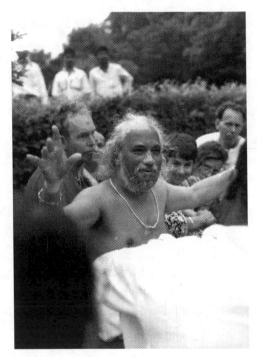

Photo by Peter A. Geniesse

Guru Sant Keshavadas leads Hindu pilgrims to the sacred shrines in the high Himalayas in northern India after baptizing them in the Ganges River.

"I don't consider myself an orthodox Hindu. My idea was to preach universal love and peace."
—Sant Keshavadas

CHAPTER TWENTY

GURU SANT KESHAVADAS

1934-1997
Rishikesh, India   1994

The compact buses, built for mountain switchbacks, were poised for the pilgrimage. Darkness and heavy fog were rapidly descending on the Himalayan foothills across the Ganges River where elephants and tigers roam.

Rama Mata made an impassioned plea. Let's stay the night in Rishikesh, she said, and travel the narrow, pocked mountain road so often plagued by mudslides in daylight. The pilgrims were nervous, but they didn't say a word.

Her husband, Sant Keshavadas, 60, a Hindu guru from southern India who spent almost half of his life in the West, listened and then softly said, "Let's pray."

He chanted praises to the Hindu deities. *"Aum Namah Sivaya."* The pilgrims responded to the Sanskrit litany.

Then he said, "Let's go."

Three buses inched up the shrouded pass as hundreds of wild monkeys frolicked along the side of the road. In another 10 minutes, the military would close the mountain route for the night.

It was time to test the gods -- and the faith of the pilgrims who rattled their prayer beads each time when their bus slid toward the abyss of a switchback or bucked a mudslide.

Keshavadas had been there before. In the 25 years he had lived in the United States, he had led 17 pilgrimages to the sacred shrines of India.

For most of the pilgrims, however, it was a strange spiritual journey. Sixty Westerners, most from the United States – physicians and psychics, retired school teachers and teenagers, latter day hippies and business executives – were following their guru to the font of their new faith.

Some were Hindus, born and raised in the Indian culture, who were living in the United States. Others could never be. The religion accepts no converts.

No matter. They sported red marks on their foreheads – the *tilaka*, the third eye of enlightenment – and they called each other by their adopted religious names. They fingered their prayer beads and mumbled in Sanskrit.

For some, the pilgrimage fulfilled lifelong spiritual dreams. For others it was a grueling tour in squalid conditions to be recounted but never to be repeated.

Keshavadas knew the faith of pilgrims was best tested in adversity. "A pilgrimage is the greatest spiritual discipline for self-transformation," he said.

Shortly after midnight, the buses chugged into Uttarkashi on the banks of the Upper Ganges. The trek with the gods of the world's oldest religion was underway. For the next 10 days, the pilgrims increasingly were put to the test by Eastern spirituality, the strange *sadhus*, the ancient temples and the treacherous terrain along the sacred river high in the Himalayas.

They forded streams when rock avalanches wiped out roads and they climbed mountains in downpours and in the dark of night to reach the cave of the *Babaji*, the ever-living master. They were on the river at dawn in Varanasi as thousands ritually bathed in the swollen, polluted Ganges. They watched in horror the flames of the funeral pyres along the shore and the bloated dead bodies tumbling in the current.

For many, it was bizarre, the source of recurring nightmares. The anguished lepers who begged with outstretched stubs. The haunting painted faces of holy men who lives in caves. The hollow eyes of starving children.

For some it was a deeply mystical journey into the world's most spiritual land.

For Keshavadas – known simply by tens of thousands devotees as *Guruji* – it was his final West-to-East pilgrimage. After the Himalayan trek, he returned to Bangalore in southern India.

In July, 1994, tens of thousands attended the inauguration of Bhagavadgita Temple and Gayatri University, funded in large part by his American disciples.

Back in the late 1960s, he founded the Temple of Cosmic Religion in Oakland, Calif., where he fostered an ecumenical, universal spirituality.

"God is one; many are his names," was his calling card.

He's the author of 20 books, the producer of 600 inspirational cassettes and the composer of 6,000 spiritual songs.

He's known by millions in India and in the metropolitan areas of America and Europe where he established yoga centers. He regularly lectured in London, Paris, Munich and Israel. In the summer of 1993, he was one of eight major religious figures to address the second Parliament of World Religions in Chicago.

His appearance came a century after Hinduism was first introduced in the West by Swami Vivecananda at the first Parliament of World Religions in Chicago. "Americans had the insight of seeing the greatest of Himalayan wisdom in this man," he said.

Keshavadas was a Hindu spiritual leader ever since he was a boy tending cattle on the southern Indian countryside. When he was 11, he had a mystical white light experience that redeemed his life. He heard a voice say, "Sing my name throughout the world." He became the singing saint.

He was the third oldest in an upper-caste family of nine. He went to law school but he couldn't shake his religious calling.

In 1966 Keshavadas made the *Kumbh Mela* at Allahabad, which he called "the greatest spiritual gathering in India." An estimated 30 million people took part in the sacred rituals of the Ganges. It was there that he met the *Babaji,* the ever-living master, the holy man of the Himalayas who lived 500 years ago.

The *Babaji*, according to legend, resided in a simple cave in the foothills of Nanda Devi, the Hindu's sacred mountain. But that day the *avatar* – heralded in the West in Paramhansa Yogananda's "Autobiography of a Yogi" – appeared to Keshavadas in Allahabad as a tall, naked man.

Keshavadas recalled the *Babaji* asking: "What are you doing here? You have a big job to do in the West."

He then set out on a speaking tour. He lectured in Germany, in London and New York before settling in northern California.

"I don't consider myself an orthodox Hindu," he said. "My idea was not to teach Hinduism but rather to preach universal love and peace."

Keshavadas spoke in churches and synagogues. He met with Pope Paul VI and Mother Teresa. He taught Buddhism and Jainism. "All religions are true," he said. "All bibles are the inspiration of the same Lord."

But while he lectured throughout the world, and reached millions more through his writings, he remained especially fond of leading small pilgrimages to the sacred sites of northern India.

"A pilgrimage is beautiful," he said. "You can offer up at a holy place your sins, karma, anger and go back light-hearted." Besides, he said, the blessings from such a trip goes a long way as a contribution to world peace. "This has been my on-going effort to bring the East and the West together."

Keshavadas performed *pujas* in centuries-old temples. He baptized his devotees in the sacred Ganges, in its cold mountain waters and in the chocolate-brown contaminated flow hundreds of miles downstream.

He gathered his disciples on grassy slopes, in *ashrams*, in Hindu temples and Buddhist *stupas* to speak of love and peace in song and parables drawn from the Old and New Testaments, from the Vedas and from the Koran.

And he climbed the mountain, with 50 of his devotees, in a summer downpour to make one last visit to the cave of the *Babaji*.

He then retired to his center for Hindu studies in Bangalore, satisfied with his life-long efforts toward peace and religious unity.

"I never was like other gurus. I never developed a cult," he said. "Many of those who have heard me have become teachers and healers and some have formed their own centers.

"I'm proud I was an inspiration to any school of thought to bring this work of health and healing to humanity."

Keshavadas died in 1997 at the age of 67. Before he died, he empowered his wife, Rama Mata, with the guru lineage. She was a devoted disciple-servant during their 46 years of marriage.

Guru Mata is president of the Temple of Cosmic Religion in California and continues to administer its world headquarters at Vishwa Shanti Ashrama in Bangalore, India.

Badrinath, India – It's 5 a.m. and the ancient temple loudspeakers crackles the wakeup call.

The litany of the 1001 names for the Lord Vishnu is being chanted over the scratchy recording. The beggars take their appointed places on the temple steps and line up along the railing of the bridge spanning the roaring mountain river called Alaknanda.

Steam rises from the nearby thermal pools where pilgrims soak before entering the temple for the *puja* rituals of daybreak.

It's cold and damp at 10,000 feet at the Himalayas' greatest shrine.

Badrinath, nestled amid peaks topping 25,000 feet, and reachable by a precarious, one-lane road narrowed by landslides, draws tens of thousands of visitors each summer.

A few never return to their homes. Badrinath is where they go to die.

It's one of four major shrines – Yamunotri, Gangotri and Kedarnath are the others – high in the mountains where the Ganges River picks up its flow.

To Hindus, the Himalayas and the Ganges are where the gods reside. It's where pilgrims can wash away their sins. It's where *"moksha,"* the last incarnation, can be pursued.

It's about 200 miles from the "Gateway to the Gods" in the Ganges plain to Badrinath, and while buses, trucks and taxis regularly wind their way up the valley slopes, many pilgrims prefer to process on foot, carrying ornate vessels to return Ganges water to their villages.

Hardiwar and nearby Rishikesh, "The Yoga Capital of the World," are the staging areas for most pilgrimages to mountain shrines. Rishikesh, which claims scores of *ashrams*, gained fleeting fame in the 1960s when the Beatles arrived to consult with their Transcendental Meditation guru, Maharisi Mahesh Yogi.

Thousands of Westerners still flock to Rishikesh to study yoga and Hinduism from the Masters on the banks of the Ganges. The Divine Life Society, founded by Swami Shivananda in 1936, has a major presence among the scores of *ashrams*, and hundreds of *swamis* and *sadhus* which take part in the *satsanga* ceremonies.

But while the densely populated Ganges plains draw the masses, the high Himalayan shrines with their spectacular backdrops of snow-covered peaks, glaciers and cascading rivers, are the destination of the true pilgrims.

Badrinath lies above the Valley of the Flowers, a six-mile long oasis which has been turned into a national park. Its clarion call is the bell of the ancient temple with Buddhist influences from another era on the banks of the Alaknanda River.

There, ever since the 7th century, the same clan of Brahmin priests from southern India has presided over spirited ceremonies from dawn to dusk for thousands of worshipers. They chant the litanies of the saints, clang bells and cymbals and offer *prasad*, handfuls of symbolic food, to the gods of a dozen altars.

The pilgrims hike the muddy trails during the summer monsoon season. Winter's snow seals off the region. They stay in *ashrams* and *dharamsalas* or in the homes of Sikhs for weeks, spending all their savings to fulfill their life's mission of shedding sins and attaining salvation.

Some never return to their villages. The old-timers like to say they're "forever trekking."

Wherever there are sacred sites, there are Hindu pilgrims. And wherever there are pilgrims, there are *sadhus* and beggars who make a living, albeit meager, off of alms.

The *sadhus* are considered holy men on a spiritual mission who wear their devoted gods' colors on their foreheads while they ponder the mysteries in mountain caves. There are thousands of them. Many are true hermits but some are just societal dropouts looking for a handout.

The beggars are more bothersome. Some are blind, others lame, and many are missing fingers and toes to leprosy – and to the knife. They present a pathetic portrait of Indian's poor everywhere along the religious tourist route.

They line the steps of the temples, the bathing *ghats*, the markets and bazaars wrapped in rags with tin cups in hand.

They, too, are an institution. They serve the faith by allowing Hindus to accumulate good karma just by giving a few coins.

In front of the temples, moneychangers will convert a dime into a handful of near-useless tin tokens so pilgrims can drop one in each beggar's cup before entering the gate to take part in *puja* ceremonies.

One bone-chilling dawn at Badrinath, as beggars took their places on the temple steps, I stopped by a vendor to get a cup of hot tea. One shivering leper pleaded with his eyes. So I bought him a cup. Three other beggars glanced my way.

Give them tea, too, I said. What about those others? The vendor asked. A round of hot tea for all my friends, I said. I sat on the temple steps and toasted the morning's sunrise with a dozen beggars.

You rarely see a beggar smile. But later that day as passing pilgrims dropped pieces of tin in their cups, one looked up at me, nodded and grinned.

Peter A. Geniesse

Resources:

Peter A. Geniesse, "Trek with the Gods," The Post-Crescent, Appleton, WI, Sept. 5, 1994.

Maryknoll Magazine, "Baptism in the Ganges," Maryknoll, N.Y., June, 1995.

Encyclopedia of Hinduism, "Keshavadas, Sant," Temple of Cosmic Religion, 1997.

CHAPTER TWENTY-ONE

Photo by Peter A. Geniesse
The 14th Dalai Lama, in exile from his base in Tibet, also was banned from the revered birthplace of Siddhartha Gautama Buddha in Nepal and the centuries old stupa of Swayambhunath In Kathmandu.

"Sometime in 2025, when I'm 90, the 14th Dalai Lama will consult with the High Lamas of the Tibetan Buddhist Tradition to determine whether I'll have a successor."
—Tenzen Gyatso

CHAPTER TWENTY-ONE

THE 14TH DALAI LAMA

1935—
Kathmandu, Nepal   1994

Buddhism's most famous disciple alive was not welcome in the birthplace of Buddha back in 2010.

The Dalai Lama's 75th birthday was observed without ceremony at the Tibetan Refugee Camp in Nepal. In fact 350 Tibetan followers were detained by Nepal police for trying to pray for his long life. They weren't permitted to attend ceremonies at the traditional Buddhists' centuries-old stupas of Boudhanath, Swayambhunath or Pharping.

The Chinese wouldn't allow it.

The Dalai Lama only once has been able to visit Lumbini in southern Nepal, the revered birthplace of Siddhartha Gautama Buddha who was born six centuries before Christ. That was in 1987. He's preached Buddha's message all over the world, except at the religion's venerated font.

Nepal's president, Dr. Ram Baran Yadav, had accepted invitations to attend celebrations at a Buddhist monastery but was hurriedly forced to cancel them after the Chinese Embassy in Kathmandu objected fiercely. Members of Nepal's parliament also were forbidden to attend the ceremony at the refugee camp.

Such is the political clout, the intimidation and China's lingering animosity toward Tibetan Buddhists and the Dalai Lama.

The north of Nepal, adjoining Tibet, had remained restive since the 1950s after China invaded and captured Tibet, forcing the Dalai Lama, Tenzin Gyatso, to flee secretly to India after a failed uprising by Tibetans in 1959.

Tibetan warriors, trained by the CIA and India, continued to resist Chinese occupation by making quick attacks from Mustang in northern Nepal. The resistance stopped after the Dalai Lama, realizing the futility of the forays, sent word to the loyal Khampa warriors to end the guerrilla war.

The gesture saved Nepal from China's wrath and possible retaliation. Nepal's King Birendra then allowed Tibetan refugees to proceed to India through Nepal. Thousands of refugees, including the Dalai Lama, resettled in Dharamsala in northern India.

For more than 30 years, the Dalai Lama has struggled to free his people from Chinese occupation. He took his case to the United Nations and was supported three times. He proposed a five-point peace plan for Tibet before the U.S. Congress in 1987 and the following year he addressed members of the European parliament.

In 1989 he was awarded the Nobel Peace Prize for his non-violent struggle for the liberation of Tibet. He has consistently advocated policies of non-violence, even in the face of extreme aggression. He also was the first Nobel Laureate to be recognized for his concern for global environment problems.

He has traveled to more than 67 countries spanning six continents in his pursuit of peace and justice, not just for Tibet but for the world. Among his favorite forums is the University of Wisconsin at Madison which he visited nine times between 1979 and 2013.

Madison became the U.S. center for Tibetan Buddhism with the 1967 arrival of Geshe Lhundub Sopa, a long-time friend and colleague of Tenzin Gyatso. Sopa joined the UW-faculty as instructor in the newly formed Buddhist studies program.

Geshe Sopa, an internationally revered Buddhist teacher, founded the Deer Park Buddhist Center near Madison in 1975. Six years later the center moved into a $6 million temple in the Village of Oregon, 10 miles south of Madison. He's the abbot, and there are six monks in residence. Madison claims at least 15 Buddhist groups and centers in its vicinity.

During an appearance in Madison, the Dalai Lama teamed up with university researchers, neuroscience professor Richard Davidson and Jonathon Patz, director of the Global Health Institute, to explore the concepts of kindness and compassion.

The Dalai Lama has held dialogues with heads of different religions and participated in many events promoting inter-religious harmony and understanding.

He has received more than 150 awards, honorary doctorates and prizes in recognition of his message of peace, non-violence, inter-religious understanding, universal responsibility and compassion. He has also authored more than 110 books.

Since the mid-1980s, he has carried on a dialogue with modern scientists, mostly in the fields of psychology, neurobiology, quantum physics and cosmology. This has led to an historic collaboration between Buddhist monks and world-renowned scientists in trying to help individuals achieve peace of mind.

On March 14, 2011, the Dalai Lama sent a letter to the Tibetan parliament in exile requesting them to devolve him of his temporal power. According to the charter of the Tibetans in exile, His Holiness was technically still considered to be head of state.

It would bring to an end the dual spiritual and political authority of the Dalai Lama and revert to the previous tradition of the first four Dalai Lamas being just the spiritual leaders of Tibet. From 1642 to the 1950s, the Dalai Lamas or their regents headed the Tibetan government.

The democratically elected leadership would assume complete formal political leadership of Tibet. The Ganden Phodrang, the institution of the Dalai Lamas, would continue and remain intact.

On May 29, 2011, His Holiness signed into law the formal transfer of his temporal power to the democratically elected leader. This brought to an end the 368-year-old tradition of the Dalai Lamas being both spiritual and temporal head of Tibet.

As far back at 1969, His Holiness made it clear that the people should decide whether the Dalai Lama's reincarnations should continue in the future.

He was concerned that, if the people so choose to continue the sacred tradition, that "vested political interests" might misuse the reincarnation system to fulfill their own political agenda.

Clear guidelines were drawn up and adopted on Sept. 24, 2011, so that there would be "no room for doubt or deception."

His Holiness said that when he is 90, sometime in 2025, he will consult the high Lamas of the Tibetan Buddhist tradition, the Tibetan public and other concerned people who follow Tibetan Buddhism to re-evaluate whether the institution of the Dalai Lama should continue.

If it is decided that reincarnation should continue, and there is a need for the 15th Dalai Lama to be recognized, responsibility for that will rest with the officers of the Dalai Lama's Ganden Phodrang Trust.

However, there is a caveat in the selection of the next Dalai Lama. Apart from the reincarnation recognized through legitimate methods, no recognition or acceptance should be given to a candidate chosen for political ends by anyone, including those in the People's Republic of China.

Tenzen Gyatso describes himself as a simple Buddhist monk. He was born on July 6, 1935 to a farming family in a small hamlet located in Taktser, Amdo, in northeastern Tibet.

When he was two years old, he was recognized as the reincarnation of the previous 13th Dalai Lama, Thubten Gyatso.

The Dalai Lamas are believed to be manifestations of Avalokiteshvara or Chenrezig, the Bodhisattva of Compassion and the patron saint of Tibet. Bodhisattvas are believed to be enlightened beings who have postponed their own nirvana-- the Buddhists idea of heavenly peace-- and have chosen to take rebirth in order to serve humanity.

A search party was sent to locate the new incarnation. The northeast became the sector, the sacred lake of Lhamo La-tso narrowed the selection, and a one-story house with unique tiling matching the vision of the Regent favored Thondup.

The boy then was presented various relics, including toys, some of which belonged to the 13th Dalai Lama, and some that didn't. Thondup correctly identified all the items belonging to the previous Dalai Lama, exclaiming "It's mine. It's mine."

His enthronement ceremony as the Dalai Lama was held in Lhasa in 1940, and he assumed full temporal power over Tibet on Nov. 17, 1950, at the age of 15. It was right after China's invasion of Tibet.

In 1954, the teen-aged Dalai Lama went to Beijing for peace talks with Mao Zedong and other Chinese leaders, including Deng Xiaoping and Chou Enlai. In 1959, with the brutal suppression of the Tibetan national uprising in Lhasa by Chinese troops, His Holiness was forced to escape into exile. Since then he has been living in Dharamsala in northern India, where the Tibetan government in exile is located.

Throughout the Kathmandu Valley, there are hundreds of Hindu temples and Buddhist stupas, some dating back more than 2,000 years ago. It is said that Buddha was born in Nepal, south of Pokara, in the 5th century B.C. He crossed over into India for enlightenment, and seven centuries later, the Buddhist Indian emperor Ashoka returned the favor, building four stupas in the Kathmandu Valley.

Thus, while Nepal is the world's only official Hindu nation, 80 per cent claim to be Hindus, and many of its temples, traditions and practices represent a peaceful fusion of the two religions. The historic towns of Patan and Bhaktapur have squares lined with Vishnu and Siva temples, many sporting centuries-old erotic art carved on struts beneath the pagoda eaves.

Nepal also can claim its own living goddess, the Kumari Devi, a young girl who lives in a special temple off Kathmandu's Durbar Square.

She is selected for physical and spiritual perfection at age five and reigns until her first menses, when she moves out and another takes her place.

Holy men, sadhus and swamis, are stationed near most temple gates, some toying with serpents and tridents while others seeking handouts. Most stands in the bazaars sell statues of Hindu's pantheon of gods as well as elaborate Buddhist prayer wheels.

The ancient Buddhist stupa of Swayambhunath commands a hill not far from a sacred site for more than 2,000 years. Atop the giant mound, the watchful eyes of Buddha look out over the valley in four directions.

Pilgrims walk clockwise around the stupa, spinning hundreds of prayer wheels above flaming tapers while scores of monkeys frolic about the giant statues. Nearby is a Buddhist monastery, where many of the country's thousands of monks, some as young as seven years old, meditate and study.

The imposing Swayambhunath, the country's most recognized site – after Mt. Everest – also is the focal point of more than 12,000 Tibetans who settled in Nepal to escape Chinese persecution.

Nepal, home to eight of the world's 10 tallest mountains, including Mt. Everest at 29.029 feet, the highest point on earth, is a landlocked nation bordered by China on the north and India on the other three sides.

It's about the size of Wisconsin but with a population of 27 million. Kathmandu, its capital, once famed for its Freak Street, a high altitude hangout for society's dropouts, in 2010 had a population of nearly 1 million.

A 7.8 earthquake on April 26, 2015, the largest in 80 years, destroyed much of Kathmandu and its vast fertile valley, a swath measuring 17 miles long and 13 miles wide.

The death toll reached 2,100, another 1,000 were injured and tens of thousands were left homeless. The earthquake and aftershocks affected neighboring countries, killing 51 in India, and 17 in Tibet. Ten climbers and their guides died in avalanches while climbing Mt. Everest.

Lumbini, the birthplace of Siddhartha Gautama Budda in 563 B.C., is a UNESCO World Heritage Site and draws Buddhist pilgrims from throughput the world. It's considered a holy site in a monastic zone where only monasteries are permitted.

Someday, the 14th Dalai Lama, the longest reigning Lama, or guru, prays he finally will be permitted to visit the font of the Buddhist religion he aspires.

Resources:

Peter A. Geniesse, "Hindu kingdom at top of the world," *Newsday,* Dec. 10, 1994.

"Nepal still forbidden domain for Dalai Lama," The Times of India, July 6, 2010.

Doug Erickson, "Dalai Lama's visit shines light," Wisconsin State Journal, May 13, 2013.

Wikipedia, the free encyclopedia, "Dalai Lama," July 22, 2015.

CHAPTER TWENTY-TWO

Photo by Peter A. Geniesse

Food for the Poor founder Ferdinand Mahfood comforts a young girl during a mission trip to Georgetown, Guyana.

"We've had thousands of requests in the past 15 years, and we've never had to tell anyone no. The miracle of the thing it that it works."
–Ferdinand Mahfood

CHAPTER TWENTY-TWO

'BEGGAR' FERD MAHFOOD

1937-
Georgetown, Guyana   1995

He once was a wealthy Jamaican businessman, running his family's million-dollar export company. Then at age 58, he became a beggar -- for the poor.

Ferdinand Mahfood founded Food for the Poor in 1982, and within 15 years he had raised and delivered $240 million worth of rice and beans, hospital beds and school desks, among other necessities, for the desperately poor in 17 Latin American countries.

He's a good beggar. Millions of dollars flow through his Food for the Poor programs each month. And those millions have made a big impact, especially in the Caribbean.

Mahfood walked the talk, too, and everywhere he traveled, he visited the slums, assessed their greatest needs and fulfilled their promises.

On a 1995 tour of Guyana, the second poorest country in the hemisphere, next to Haiti, he visited prisons, homes for the dying, leper colonies and health hospices, heeding the desires of the poor.

At one home a woman was living with her children in a wretched hovel, smaller than a closet. He promised her a new house. It was to be a prefabricated structure measuring 12 and 24 feet, but it gave her hope.

Mahfood promised an elderly housing tenement a propane stove to replace its wood-fired one. He promised handicapped children some physical therapy equipment. Lepers at the Mahiaca Hospital were to get batteries for their transistor radios. Its chapel would get a piano.

"We're trying to identify needs," he said. "If a roof needs fixing, you can't send in clothes."

His Guyanese staffers jotted down each request and pledged to deliver the goods within months. They never have failed to fulfill an order.

One morning Mahfood pledged new 12-by-24-foot houses to 20 impoverished families. Later that same day, the pledge grew to 50 families. By the end of his four-day pilgrimage, he was attempting to find land to build more than 500 houses.

"If we could house 500 families, we could create a social revolution in Guyana," he said.

In just a few days, Mahfood had committed Food for the Poor to spending millions of dollars.

"We don't calculate what it costs," he said. "The Lord is my calculator. He keeps track of what I give."

Mahfood relied on collective Christian charity, and pointed to accounts in the Bible of the early Church when St. Paul raised funds to build churches outside of Jerusalem.

"We're going around the country trying to find people to help us build houses for the poor," he said.

"We've had thousands of requests in the past 15 years," he said. "And we've never had to tell anyone no.

"The miracle of this thing is that it works."

In the early 1970s, shortly after Mahfood took over Essex Exports from his father, he decided to do something different with his life. He started small, showing films and giving candy and comic books to poor children in Kingston, Jamaica. Later on, he offered help to missionaries.

One day on a business trip to Chicago, he read a book that his wife gave him. It was the final chapter of "Something More," by Catherine Marshall, that changed his life.

"Tears flowed out of my eyes like a river. I was reading and praying and talking to God. I was in a spiritual daze," he said.

But it wasn't until 1982 when he visited a poorhouse in Jamaica that he knew what God wanted.

"I said to God, 'if You want, I'll beg for the poor.'"

That year Food for the Poor was born in Jamaica. The agency's mission was expanded when a donor offered $10,000 for Mahfood to also serve Haiti. Its reach continued to grow, serving 17 countries by 1994, including feeding programs in Florida, New York and San Francisco. That year, the agency delivered aid valued at $32.2 million.

In the first 15 years of the ministry, Jamaica received more than $100 million in assistance. Haiti got $50 million and Guyana, $20 million. Other major recipients included the Caribbean islands of St. Lucia, Trinidad, Grenada and Dominica.

Over the past 33 years, Food for the Poor has distributed an estimated $9 billion worth of food, medicine, housing materials and other aid, much of it donated, to the needy of the Caribbean and Latin America.

It's ranked as the 66th largest charity in the United States, larger than UNICIF and CARE. It employs a staff of 350 at its headquarters in Coconut Beach, Fla., and at its in-country offices. As of 2011, more than 96 percent of all donations went directly to programs that help the poor.

In 2002, when he became incapacitated, Mahfood was succeeded as president and CEO of the agency by his brother, Robin.

Guyana was originally colonized by the Netherlands in the 17th century. Later it became a British colony, known as British Guiana, and remained so for more than 150 years. It achieved independence on May 26, 1966.

Mahfood said that was when the tiny nation took a turn for the worse. The literacy rate dropped from 95 percent to 65 percent by 1995. The per capita income then was about a dollar a day.

The World Bank has rated Guyana as one of the poorest countries in the hemisphere, comparable to Haiti, which has had more publicity about its problems.

Because few people are aware of the poverty in Guyana, the country receives relatively little help from international relief agencies. The poverty is split between urban slums and indigent farming communities that have poor health and educational facilities.

The problems faced by these groups differ in regard to transportation and land availability. The rural poor have access to land for crops and building small homes, but they have a difficult time moving around and making use of government services. The urban poor face the opposite situation, and families often live in crowded, unsanitary conditions.

The economy of Guyana is closely tied to the nation's sugar industry, which supports about 80 percent of the population. Most of these low-paying jobs involve hard work in the fields. With a minimum wage of 50 cents, many people find it difficult to afford transportation to and from work.

Georgetown, the nation's capital, has a population of 235,000. It's called "The Garden City of the Caribbean," and is the retail, finance and administrative center of the country. It's on the Atlantic Ocean, at the mouth of the Demerara River estuary. The city is about three feet below sea level at high tide, and sea and retaining walls, along with a network of canals, control the flow.

Guyana – "Land of Many Waters" -- has a population of 850,000, with most of the people living in the northern third of the country. East Indians, who migrated to Guyana as indentured servants at the turn of the 20th century, represent 43 percent. Blacks, descendants of African slaves, have about the same number. Amerindians, 11 tribes clustered along rivers speaking distinct languages, amount to about 10 percent.

Guyana has nominated Kaieteur National Park and its spectacular waterfalls and its giant jungle vegetation to UNESCO as a first World Heritage Site. The falls, the world's highest of sustained flow, tumbles 741 feet, or five times that of U.S. Niagara Falls.

Christopher Columbus had Guyana in his sights during his third voyage in 1498. Spanish conquistadores casually overlooked its jungles as a likely source in their search for El Dorado. It wasn't until the 1990s before the golden bonanza was uncovered.

In 1993, Omai Gold Mines, a consortium between Canadian company Cambior and the government of Guyana, operated the largest open pit gold mine in the world about 150 miles south of Georgetown. It had estimated reserves of 3.7 million ounces of gold.

The company employed 1,000 workers in the remote northwestern corner of Guyana called Coyuni-Masaruni. Then disaster struck.

I was on the scene as a reporter on Aug. 19, 1995, when a tailings dam was breached, sending 120 million gallons of cyanide-bearing tailings into the Omai River, a tributary of the Essequibo River, the primary source of water for much of the population.

Guyana's president, Cheddi Jagan, declared much of the Essequibo an environmental disaster zone. A $2 billion class action lawsuit was filed against the company, later to be dismissed by a Guyana Supreme Court justice.

Before it closed down in 2005 after 13 years of operation, the mine produced its projected 3.7 million ounces of gold.

The spill generated international headlines and is still cited by environmentalists of the danger of using cyanide in mining operations, and the disposal of heavy metals in mine tailings.

Guyana's reputation has been scared by cyanide. Most people call to mind the English-speaking, South American country by a single word: Jonestown.

It was back in November, 1978, when more than 900 Americans died of intentional cyanide poisoning in northwestern Guyana.

The poisoning in Jonestown followed the murder of five others, notably U.S. Congressman Leo Ryan, who had come to Guyana to check up on Jim Jones and his Peoples Temple Agricultural Project.

Jones called the deaths "revolutionary suicide." Others, including Jonestown survivors, called it mass murder.

The Peoples Temple was formed in Indianapolis, Ind., during the mid-1950s. Though its roots and teachings shared more with biblical church than with Marxism, it purported to practice what it called "apostolic socialism."

In the early 1960s, Jones visited Guyana – then still a British colony –while on his way to establishing a short-lived temple mission in Brazil. In the mid-1970s, the Temple moved its headquarters to San Francisco. Unlike other figures considered as cult leaders, Jones enjoyed public support and contact with some of the highest level politicians in the U.S.

In the fall of 1973, after critical newspapers articles and the defection of eight Temple members, Jones prepared an "immediate action" contingency plan for responding to a police crackdown. For its "Caribbean missionary post," the Temple chose Guyana because it was a predominantly Indian, English-speaking socialist country which would "afford Black members of the Temple a peaceful place to live."

The Temple negotiated a lease of 3,800 acres of jungle land located 150 miles west of Georgetown. Some 500 members began the construction of the settlement. Jones saw it as a "socialist paradise" and a "sanctuary" from media scrutiny.

After mass migration, Jonestown became overcrowded. Its population was just under 1,000 at its peak in 1978. Up to $65,000 in monthly welfare payments from U.S. government agencies were signed over to the Temple. Jones had access to $26 million that year.

As defectors told of nightmarish experiences, and media accounts questioned the veracity of the cult, Jones became increasingly paranoid that the CIA and the "capitalist pigs" were out to destroy Jonestown. He initiated "White Nights" to pose and practice severe alternatives in such a case. His choices included fleeing to the Soviet Union, committing "revolutionary suicide," fighting the purported attackers or heading off into the jungle.

"Revolutionary suicide" became the option and simulated mass suicides were rehearsed. The slide into madness was accompanied by Jones' deteriorating health and deep-seated persecution complex, paranoia and megalomania.

The Temple had received monthly half-pound shipments of cyanide since 1976 after Jones obtained a jeweler's license to buy the chemical, ostensibly to clean gold.

Congressman Ryan, along with a delegation of 18 people, including several San Francisco area newsmen, flew to Jonestown in response to his constituents' concerns. Upon his return from the compound, he was assassinated, setting off the rehearsed self-murder by cyanide and Cool Aid of hundreds of children.

Jones was found dead of apparent self-inflicted gunshot wounds.

Twenty-five years later, the burned out compound that was Jonestown had been reclaimed by the jungle.

Several months before I visited Guyana in 1995 with Ferdinand Mahfood and his Food for the Poor contingent, I was in Haiti on a freelance assignment to see how the country was faring under the United Nations' peacekeeping mission.

It was a different place from what I had witnessed two years earlier. In 1993, when the military was in command, along with remnants of the feared *Tontons Macoute*, foreigners, especially Caucasians, held favored status.

My Black Haitian friends often reminded me that "they don't kill white men." To do so would bring down the wrath of the U.S., they said. They do and did, however, murder hundreds of their own kind. No Black man who spoke fondly of Jean-Bertrand Aristide was safe in his own country.

But for me, I carried a certain voodoo for protection. I traveled alone in Tap-Taps taxis and in the back of trucks in Port-au-Prince and throughout the country, with apprehension but not fear.

Two years later, thousands of United Nations' peacekeepers had corralled the military regime, and had curtailed the political killings. No longer were bodies with dire messages pinned to their chests found on the sidewalks of the capital. The killings hadn't stopped; only the victims had changed. Now the motive was simply economic, rather than political, the United Nations' spokesman reported.

I was in Port-au-Prince to flesh out a story on Food for the Poor's outstanding feeding program where thousands of poor Haitians stood in line for their only meals of the day.

I took a Tap-Tap to the end of the paved road, and started walking along a dusty path in scorching temperatures toward Food for the Poor's headquarters. I encountered groups of young men, lingering in the shade of a cluster of sparse trees.

I sensed my voodoo had worn off. So I engaged one group of six in trite conversation in my limited French-Creole as they circled about me. I asked them if they knew the way to the agency's headquarters and they said they would show me.

The three-story building was but a block away. I could see it in the distance. They insisted that they accompany me. I assumed they wanted money. When we arrived at Food for Poor's headquarters, I thanked them and gave them some change.

I thought they would disperse, but three hours later, as I left the building they were waiting for me. They wanted my camera, my wallet, my passport, and if I resisted, my life. The six pinned me to the ground, struck me in the face and groin. I struggled to keep hold of my camera bag and documents, but I was losing the battle and I was bloody and hurting.

There were witnesses in the area, but they looked the other way. Just as I was about to release my grip, a white van pulled up, my assailants scattered and two Black men pulled me into the van.

I asked if they were angels. No, they said, they just worked for Food for the Poor. They saw me flailing about from a third floor window, and realized that White guys with money were now Haiti's victims of choice.

Resources:

Peter A. Geniesse, "He Begs for the Poor;" Sunday Digest, Colorado Springs, CO, May 1997.

Wikipedia, the free encyclopedia; "Food for the Poor," June 22, 2015.

Source Watch, "Omai Gold Mines; Oct. 20, 2012.

Kenneth D. MacHarq, "Agency Founder Resigns"; Christianity Today, Oct. 5, 2002.

Wikipedia, the free encyclopedia; "Jamestown," July14, 2015.

CHAPTER TWENTY-THREE

Photo by Peter A. Geniesse

Father Bill Brennan, S.J., processes with the cross of his friend and Jesuit martyr in El Salvador at the School of the Americas at Fort Benning, GA, in 2004. Protesters of the U.S. role in training Latin American military continue to rally around the assassinations of Archbishop Oscar Romero and other Catholic clerics.

"As a Christian, I do not believe in death without resurrection.
If they kill me, I will rise again in in the Salvadoran people."
—Oscar Romero

CHAPTER TWENTY-THREE

OSCAR ROMERO'S 'VOICE'

1917-1980
San Salvador, El Salvador   1996

He spoke for those who could not do so for themselves. In a country whose rulers regarded dissent as subversion, he used the moral authority of his office to give a voice to the voiceless.

Archbishop Oscar Romero spoke out against El Salvador's incipient civil war and the deep-rooted patterns of abuse and injustice which bred it. For that he was assassinated. But not silenced.

He had a premonition that someday he'd be killed for opening his mouth. He was willing to die, he said, if his death would contribute to the solution of his nation's problems.

"As a Christian," he said, "I do not believe in death without resurrection. If they kill me, I will rise again in the Salvadoran people."

On March 24, 1980, Romero participated in a day of recollection about the endangered priesthood, organized by Opus Dei. That evening, as he was celebrating Mass in the chapel of La Divina Providencia Hospital, he was fatally shot at the altar.

It was just one day after a sermon when he called upon Salvadoran soldiers, as Christians, to obey God's higher order and to stop carrying out the government's repression and violations of basic human rights.

Romero was buried in the Metropolitan Cathedral of San Salvador on March 30. His funeral drew an estimated 250,000 mourners from all over the world, the largest demonstration in Salvadoran history.

During the ceremony, smoke bombs exploded in the streets near the cathedral and gunshots came from the National Palace. As many as 50 were killed by gunfire and in the stampede of people running away from the explosions.

At the funeral, Cardinal Ernesto Carripio y Ahumada, the personal delegate of Pope John Paul II, eulogized Romero as a "beloved, peace-making man of God," adding that "his blood will give fruit to brotherhood, love and peace."

Oscar Arnulfo Romero y Galdámez was born in Ciudad Barrios, El Salvador, on Aug. 15, 1917. His father apprenticed him to a carpenter when he was 13 but Oscar sensed a vocation to the priesthood and left home the following year to enter the seminary. He studied in El Salvador and at the Gregorian University in Rome where he was ordained a priest in 1942.

Romero spent the first 25 years of his ministerial career as a parish priest. He later was named rector of the seminary and became secretary of the Bishops' Conference and director of the archdiocesan newspaper. He was considered conservative as editor, defending the traditional magisterium of the Catholic Church.

In 1970, he became auxiliary bishop of San Salvador, and then was named bishop of the Diocese of Santiago de Maria, a poor, rural region. In February 1977, he was appointed archbishop of San Salvador.

While this appointment was welcomed by the government, many priests were disappointed. The progressive priests feared that his conservative reputation would negatively affect liberation theology's commitment to the poor.

Romero's rise to prominence in the Catholic hierarchy coincided with a period of dramatic change in the Church in Latin America. The region's bishops meeting at Medellin, Colombia, in 1968 to discuss local implementation of the Second Vatican Council (1962-65) had resolved to abandon the hierarchy's traditional role as defender of the status quo and to side, instead, with the poor in their struggle for social justice.

This radical departure divided both the faithful and the clergy.

During this period, Romero was considered a conservative, even a skeptic of Vatican II reforms and the Medellin pronouncements. Thus, his appointment as archbishop in 1977 was not popular with the socially committed clergy, who feared it signaled the Vatican's desire to restrain them.

To their surprise, Romero emerged almost immediately as an outspoken opponent of injustice and a defender of the poor.

During his brief tenure as bishop of Santiago de Maria, he witnessed the suffering of El Salvador's landless poor. He witnessed increasing government violence against socially committed priests and laypersons. It led him to fear that the Church, itself, was under attack.

The assassination of his long-time friend, Jesuit Father Rutilio Grande, who had been creating self-reliance groups among the poor, just weeks after he became archbishop, had a profound impact on Romero.

"When I looked at Rutilio lying there dead," he said, "I thought if they had killed him for doing what he did, then I, too, have to walk the same path.'"

Romero urged government officials to investigate, but they ignored his request. Furthermore, the censored press remained silent.

Rutilio's death brought a stinging denunciation from Romero, who suspended Masses in the capital's churches the following Sunday and demanded the punishment of the responsible parties.

In 1979, the Revolutionary Government Junta came to power amid a wave of human rights abuses by paramilitary right-wing groups and the government in an escalation of violence that would become the Salvadoran Civil War.

Romero criticized the United States for giving military aid to the new government and wrote to President Jimmy Carter in February 1980, warning that increased U.S. military aid would "undoubtedly sharpen the injustice and the political repression inflicted on the organized people, whose struggle has often been for their most basic rights."

Carter, concerned that El Salvador would become "another Nicaragua," ignored Romero's pleas and continued military aid to the Salvadoran government.

Romero's campaign for human rights in El Salvador won him many national and international admirers, as well as a Noble Peace Prize nomination. He was given an honorary doctorate from the University of Louvain. While he was in Europe to receive the honor, he met with Pope John Paul II who expressed concern about what was happening in El Salvador.

Romero argued that it was problematic to support the Salvadoran government because it legitimized terror and assassinations.

As Romero spoke out more and more frequently, he gathered a popular following who crowded into the cathedral to hear him preach or listened to his sermons over the archdiocesan radio station. In his sermons, among other things, he listed disappearances, tortures and murders. This was followed by an hour-long speech the next day. His radio discourses drew the largest audiences in the country.

Romero denounced the persecution of members of the Catholic Church who had worked on behalf of the poor. In his speech at Louvain, Belgium, on Feb. 2, 1980, he said that more than 50 priests had been attacked. The Catholic radio station and educational institutions have been threatened, and parish communities had been raided.

"There have been threats, arrests, tortures, murderers, numbering in the hundreds, thousands," he said.

"But it's important to note why the Church has been persecuted. That part of the Church has been attacked and persecuted that put itself on the side of the people and went to the people's defense.

"Here again we find the same key to understanding the persecution of the Church: the poor."

Six weeks later, Archbishop Oscar Romero was dead, by an assassin's bullet.

To date, no one has ever been prosecuted for the assassination. In 2010, Alvaro Saravia named Roberto D'Aubuisson as giving the assassination order to him over the phone.

Saravia said he drove the assassin to the chapel and paid him 1,000 Salvadoran colons after the event. The assassin has not been identified.

It is widely believed that the assassins were members of a death squad led by former Major D'Aubuisson. That's supported by former U.S. ambassador Robert White who in a 1986 report to U.S. Congress that "there was sufficient evidence" to convict D'Aubuisson of planning and ordering Archbishop Romero's assassination.

D'Aubuisson later founded the political party, Nationalist Republican Alliance (ARENA), and organized death squads that systematically carried out politically motivated assassinations and other human rights abuses in El Salvador.

Alvaro Saravia, former captain in the Salvadoran Air Force, was chief of security for D'Aubuisson and an active member of the death squads. In 2003 a U.S. human rights organization filed a civil action against Saravia. He was found liable for aiding, conspiring and participating in the assassination of Romero. He was ordered to pay $10 million for "extrajudicial killing" and crimes against humanity.

On March 24, 2010, the 30th anniversary of Romero's death, Salvadoran President Mauricio Funes offered an official state apology for Romero's assassination. Speaking before Romero's family, representatives of the Catholic Church, diplomats and government officials, Funes said those involved in the assassination "unfortunately acted with the protection, collaboration or participation of state agents."

In 1990, on the 10th anniversary of his assassination, Romero's cause for beatification and eventual canonization was initiated. Pope John Paul II approved the first step, "Servant of God," in 1997, but then the cause stalled. Pope Benedict XVI reopened the case in 2012 and Pope Francis cut through the bureaucracy by declaring Romero a martyr, paving the way for Romero's beatification.

The Congregation for Saints' Causes recognized Romero as a martyr, stating "He was killed at the altar. Through him they wanted to strike the Church that flowed from the Second Vatican Council."

Romero's assassination was caused, they declared, "by hatred for a faith that, imbued with charity, would not be silent in the face of the injustices that relentlessly and cruelly slaughtered the poor and their defenders."

The beatification of Romero took place in San Salvador on May 23, 2015, in the Plaza Salvador del Mundo. A crowd estimated at 250,000 attended the service, many watching on large television screens set up in the streets around the plaza.

The rape and murder of four U.S. missionary women, Dec. 2, 1980

Jean Donovan was a big fan of Archbishop Oscar Romero. She often went to the Catedral Metropolitana de San Salvador to hear him preach. After his assassination on March 24, 1980, she and Sister Dorothy Kazel stood beside his coffin during the night-long vigil of his wake.

Jean and Sister Dorothy, an Ursuline nun, worked in a Catholic parish in La Libertad, serving the refugees of the Salvadoran civil war. They provided shelter, food, transportation to medical care, and they buried the bodies of the dead left behind by the death squads.

Jean was born into an upper-middle class family in Westport, Connecticut, completed her master's degree in business from Case Western Reserve University, and was engaged to a young physician.

While volunteering in the Cleveland Diocese's youth ministry with the poor, she decided to join the diocese's mission project in El Salvador. That was in 1977. When the Peace Corps withdrew its members from the country, she was ready to leave, too. Except, she said she couldn't abandon the children, "the poor, bruised victims of this insanity."

In the afternoon of Dec. 2, 1980, she and Sister Dorothy drove to the airport in San Salvador to pick up two Maryknoll missionaries – Sisters

Maura Clark and Ita Ford – who had attended a conference in Managua, Nicaragua.

They were under surveillance by a National Guardsman, who phoned his commander for orders. Five Guardsmen, in civilian clothes, were assigned to monitor their movement.

The men stopped the missionaries' vehicle as it left the airport, ordered the women out of their van and marched them to an isolated area where they beat, raped and murdered the four women.

As news of the murders was made public in the United States, public outrage forced the U.S. government to pressure the El Salvador regime to investigate. U.S. foreign policy, which had shored up the right-wing government through the Carter, Reagan and Bush administrations, was forced into the public eye.

In 1984, four National Guardsmen — Daniel Canales Ramirez, Carlos Joaquin Contreras, Francisco Orlando Contreras and José Roberto Moreno — were convicted of murdering the four missionary women and were sentenced to 30 years in prison. Their superior, Sgt. Luis Antonio Colindras, also was convicted in the slayings.

The United Nations' Truth Commission concluded that the abductions were planned in advance and that the men responsible had carried out the murders on orders from above.

The head of the National Guard, Gen. Carlos Eugenio Vides, went on to become minister of defense in the government. Later he emigrated to the U.S. and was sued by the families of the four women in federal civil court. Vides was deported to El Salvador on April 8, 2015, to face charges for various war crimes that occurred under his command.

800 civilians slain by military in El Mazote massacre of Dec. 11, 1981

The Salvadoran Civil War, a conflict between the military-led government and the Farabundo Marti National Liberation Front (FMLN), a coalition of five left-wing guerrilla groups, lasted for 12 years, from 1979 to 1992, and resulted in the deaths of at least 75,000 people. An unknown number of people "disappeared" during the conflict.

The full-fledged civil war saw extreme violence from both sides. It also included deliberate terrorizing and targeting of civilians by death squads, the recruitment of child soldiers and other violations of human rights, mostly by the military.

El Mazote, a tiny village in the Morazán department, was largely evangelical Protestant — and neutral -- unlike its Catholic neighbors who were more sympathetic to the guerrillas' cause.

On the afternoon of Dec. 10, units of the Salvadoran army's Atlacatl Battalion arrived in the remote village after a clash with guerrillas in the vicinity. Atlacatl was a "Rapid Deployment Infantry Battalion," trained by U.S. military advisors for counter-insurgency warfare.

Its mission was to eliminate the rebel presence in northern Morazán where the FMLN had a camp and training center. Upon arrival, the soldiers found not only the residents of the village but also *campesinos* who had sought refuge from the surrounding area.

The village's wealthiest man, Marcos Diaz, had gathered the citizens to warn them that the army would soon pass through the area in a counterinsurgency operation, but that he had been assured that the town's residents would not be harmed if they remained in place.

Concerned that fleeing the village would cause them to be mistaken for guerrillas, the townspeople elected to stay, and extended an offer of protection to peasants from the surrounding area who soon flooded the village.

The soldiers ordered everyone out of their houses and into the village square. They made them lie face-down, searched them and questioned them about the guerrillas. Then they ordered the villagers to lock themselves into their houses until the next day, warning that anyone coming out would be shot.

Early the next morning, the soldiers reassembled the entire village in the square. They separated the men from the women and children and locked them in separate quarters. They proceeded to interrogate, torture and execute the men in several locations. Then they began taking the women, raping some and machine-gunning all. Then they killed the children.

After killing the entire population, the soldiers set fire to the buildings.

Government officials denied that there was a massacre and U.S. officials sided with them. But on Oct. 26, 1990, a criminal complaint was filed against the Atlacatl Battalion for the massacre by Pedro Chicas Romero. He had survived the massacre by hiding in a cave above the village.

In 1992, as part of the settlement established by the Chapultepec Peace Accords signed in Mexico City, the United Nations commission supervised the exhumations of the El Mazote remains. The excavations confirmed that hundreds of civilians had been killed on the site.

In December 2011 the El Salvador government apologized for the massacre.

Six Jesuit priests murdered at Central American University, Nov. 16, 1989

Their deaths put an end to 12 years of Salvadoran uncivil war. The brutal slaying of university professors in a tiny Central American nation became a wakeup call for the world.

Tens of thousands of poor peasants had been slain in El Salvador's bloody decade. But when the military burst onto the university campus and gunned down priests who had been working for peace, the world said "enough!"

International pressure forced the Salvadoran government to sign peace agreements with the FMLN, a coalition of guerrilla groups. And the United Nation's "Truth Commission" delved into the causes and the culprits.

Father Ignacio Ellacuria, S.J., the UCA rector, and an internationally known philosopher, had played a pivotal role in negotiations for a peaceful solution to the conflict. The military targeted him for death.

The university was seen as a "refuge of subversives" by the army. Coronel Juan Orlando Zepeda, vice-minister for defense, had publicly accused UCA of being the center of operations for "FMLN terrorists," according to the Truth Commission's report.

On the evening of Nov. 15, Coronel Guillermo Alfredo Benavides informed officers under his command of the recent rebel offensive, which he termed "critical," was to be met with "full force," including using artillery and armored vehicles. Additionally, he said, "all known subversive elements were to be eliminated."

Specific orders were given to "eliminate Father Ellacuria, leaving no witnesses."

The action was to be carried out by members of the Atlacatl Battalion, an elite army unit that was created in 1980 at the U.S. Army's School of the Americas, then located in Panama.

The officers involved decided to disguise the operation as a rebel attack. The unit arrived at the UCA campus in pickup trucks. The soldiers initially tried to force their way into the Jesuits' residence until a priest let them in.

After ordering the priests to lie face-down in the back garden, the soldiers searched the residence. Then came the order to kill the priests. Soldiers firing AK-47 rifles shot and killed Father Ellacuria and five other Jesuits.

Then they shot the housekeeper and her 16-year-old daughter – twice "to finish them off."

The dead were:

> **Ignacio Ellacuria, S.J., 59, university rector and philosopher.**
> **Ignacio Martín-Baro, S.J., 44, head of psychology department.**
> **Segundo Montes, S.J., 56, head of UCA's human rights institute.**
> **Juan Ramón Moreno, S.J., 56, professor of theology.**
> **Joaquín López y López, S.J., 53, founder of schools for the poor.**
> **Amando López, S.J., 53, professor of theology.**
> **Elba Ramos, housekeeper, and her daughter Celina Ramos.**

After removing a small suitcase belonging to the priests, containing photographs, documents and $5,000, the soldiers fired machine guns, rockets and grenades at the façade of the residence.

They left a cardboard sign which read: "FMLN executed those who informed on it. Victory or death. FMLN."

Nine members of the Salvadoran military were put on trial in 1991 for the murders but there was enough evidence to convict only Col. Benavides and Lt. René Mendoza. They were sentenced to 30 years in prison but were freed on April 1, 1993, as a result of the Salvadoran Amnesty Law.

Five of the slain Jesuits were originally Spanish citizens. In 2008, a lawsuit filed in a Spanish court found 20 Salvadoran members of the military guilty of murder, terrorism and crimes against humanity.

The ruling of the Spanish court specifies that the Jesuits were murdered for having made efforts to end the Salvadoran civil war peacefully.

On the 20th anniversary of the massacre, President Mauricio Funes awarded highest government honors to the six priests. Funes was educated by the Jesuits, graduating from both Externado San José and Universidad Centroamericana. He knew the slain scholars personally, and considered some his personal friends.

The U.S. Army's School of the Americas trained El Salvador's assassins

The sun was blazing overhead as Father Bill Brennan, S.J., started out on the funeral procession outside the gates of Fort Benning, Georgia. He was in his early 80s and his health was failing.

But he couldn't miss lending his support in memory of the six Jesuits who were shot to death in El Salvador in 1989. "I knew those guys," he said. "I worked with them. I've just got to do this."

I pushed his wheelchair, held an umbrella over his head and dabbed his face with a cold cloth. We chanted "*Presente!*" to the litany of those who were slain by the Salvadoran military, many of whom had been trained at the U.S. School of the Americas.

The priests were massacred by soldiers of the elite Atlacatl Battalion, a unit created by the SOA in 1980 when it was based in Panama. It was termed a "Rapid Deployment Infantry Battalion," specially equipped for counter-insurgency warfare. It was named for an historic character who was legendary for his resistance to the Spanish conquest of Central America.

It also was implicated in some of the most infamous incidents of the Salvadoran Civil War.

Brennan served as a missionary in Belize and Honduras for 16 years before returning to Milwaukee as pastor of St. Patrick's Parish. He rarely missed the annual SOA Watch peaceful protest.

"But I've never been arrested," he said. "This time I'm going to cross the line. It's the least I can do for my brothers."

Scores of SOA protesters have been arrested and served prison time for trespassing onto the military base at Columbus, Georgia. Over the past 30 years, 183 people have served an accumulated 81 years in prison for civil disobedience. Most simply stepped across a painted line at the entrance to Fort Benning.

As we processed along with 20,000 or more holding crosses with the names of victims, we arrived at a newly installed 15-foot fence and gate.

"I can't climb over that," he said. "*Gracias a Dios!*" I said.

School of the Americas Watch, an annual vigil to protest the training of Latin American military officers, was started by Maryknoll Father Roy Bourgeois in 1983 in response to the assassination of Salvadoran Archbishop Oscar Romero, which was linked to the school's graduates.

Bourgeois was arrested in 1983 and was sentenced to 18 months in prison for trespassing on federal property. Following the murder of the six Jesuits in 1989, the protest was moved to the November anniversary date of their deaths.

In 2000, responding to "mounting protests" spearheaded by SOA Watch, the U.S. Congress renamed the School of the Americas – the Western Hemisphere Institute for Security Cooperation – rather than closing the academy.

In 2006, more than 22,000 protesters participated in the on-going effort to close down the training camp for Latin American military officers at Fort Benning.

Resources:

United Nations' publication, International Day for the Right to Truth, "Archbishop Oscar Arnulfo Romero."

Wikipedia, the free encyclopedia, "Oscar Romero," "Jean Donovan," and "Murder of UCA scholars," Aug. 2, 2015.

Patrick O'Neill, National Catholic Reporter; "SOA Watch gathers for 25th vigil," Nov. 24, 2014.

Mary Wisniewski, Reuters; "Father Bill Brennan, 92, sanctioned;" Dec. 8, 2012.

CHAPTER TWENTY-FOUR

Photo by Peter A. Geniesse

Hoa Tri Truong, 77, survived the Killing Fields of Cambodia, the Viet Kong of South Vietnam, the pirates in the Gulf of Thailand and the many family adversities after resettling in Wisconsin.

"We don't have a country. We're not Cambodian and we're not Vietnamese. We should get out of here."
–Hoa Truong

Chapter Twenty-four

'Survivor' Hoa Truong

1939 –
Kampot, Cambodia   1975

She was the matriarch of an extended family of seven, Vietnamese refugees, boatpeople who survived the communists on the mainland and pirates on the open seas.

She stood up to the Khmer Rouge of Cambodia and the Viet Cong of Vietnam. More than once she put her life on the line, insisting they either kill her or give in to her demands.

She stood a feisty four-foot-nine-inches and weighed 90 pounds. Still, she was used to having her way. She never made it past third grade, and she couldn't read or write, but when she talked, everyone listened.

Hoa Tri Truong has mellowed some over the past three decades of living in Wisconsin. She's been scarred by more than her share of adversities.

Her husband, Qui, died of emphysema at age 56 in 1987, just six years after they arrived in the U.S.

Her only daughter, Cuc, died of stomach cancer at age 32 in 1998, eleven years later.

Her only son Sang, the family's meal ticket, moved to Chicago with a girlfriend, and Kim, his former wife, remarried and took their child and her brother to Rockford, Illinois, where a cluster of Vietnamese had resettled.

Suddenly, Hoa was alone, in a tiny, dingy apartment, with her Pekinese dog named Bee-Bee and a room cluttered with plants and flowers.

Back in 1982, just one year after arriving in Neenah, Wis., Hoa and the Huynhs were living the American dream. They had moved into a five-bedroom ranch they acquired via sweat equity. They had a car and four of them had full-time jobs, albeit at minimum wage. They pooled their resources, paid their bills, and declared their independence on the 4th of July. They no longer needed refugee subsidies or support from their sponsors.

Then their dreams suddenly went south. Sang and Kim split and moved out, taking with them the mortgage payments, and the bank foreclosed on their loan.

Hoa and Qui moved into a small apartment, along with daughter Cuc.

Then Qui died. Cuc married her refugee camp sweetheart, moved to Houston where she, too, died a lingering death with her mother at her side.

Hoa was alone. "That's OK," she said in resignation.

After working for a laundry for 25 years, at minimum wage, never missing a day, and earning employee of the month and year multiple times, she was fired over a racial incident. An employee who was a Vietnam veteran goaded her on a daily basis for months and when she pushed back, they both were fired.

Then there was the traffic accident where a semi ran a red light and broadsided her car, which was turning left on a green arrow. Hoa unfairly was charged with failure to yield, lost her license and paid a hefty fine. When she recovered from her critical wounds, she said, "That's OK."

Hoa was accustomed to adversity.

Hoa Tri Truong was born in 1939, the youngest of five children, in Phnom Penh, Cambodia, the crown jewel of the French Indochinese empire. Her family was wealthy and influential. They were friends of the French. They lived in a large, two-story house on the shores of Boeng Kak.

Then her mother died. Hoa was just six years old.

Her father was a prominent businessman who owned a fleet of ships for transporting produce down the Mekong River, all the way to Saigon.

Hoa's family often was the guest of French officials, and together they toured the temples and archeological sites created by the Khmer kingdoms a thousand years earlier.

Hoa was 13 at the time, but she remembers standing in awe before the temples of Angkor Wat and envisioning the Khmers' incredible dynasty.

One year later her world came tumbling down.

In 1953, after 90 years of colonial rule, the French pulled out, Cambodia was granted its independence, and the privileged status of the Vietnamese ethnics was over.

Khmer leaders called for a boycott of foreign businessmen in Phnom Penh, many were robbed, some were killed and most Vietnamese fled to a country next door that they had never known before.

. Her family moved to Kampot, 90 miles and a five-hour drive to the south, where they had relatives. Hoa met a man who had a good job with the electric company, run by the French. On Dec. 18, 1955, she married Qui Huynh. Hoa was just 16.

In 1969, Cambodia was drawn into the Vietnam War. The U.S. had been bombing communist routes and strongholds in Laos for almost five years. Suddenly, and secretly, U.S. B-52s began carpet bombing suspected communist camps in Cambodia.

Norodom Sihanouk was just 18 when the French picked him as puppet ruler in 1941. Three decades later he was ousted by a military coup led by right-wing Gen. Lon Nol, an avowed anti-communist.

One day in August of 1970, Qui came home early from work. He had been laid off. All the Vietnamese workers had lost their jobs. They were suspected of being Viet Cong. Qui was escorted to the Kampot police station for questioning. He didn't go home for six months.

While strolling the docks in Kompong San, the country's only deep-water port, Qui met a Chinese man who understood his predicament. Chan Luu was a prosperous merchant who had been forced out of Phnom Penh. He had amassed great wealth in trade throughout Southeast Asia.

Luu had purchased a new freighter, which he named Elephant Waters, and he was looking for a good crewman. Qui signed on and was off across the Gulf of Thailand for Singapore with a cargo of sugar. One week Qui would find himself in Hong Kong and the next week in Bangkok.

Hoa and her two children remained close to their home. They were lonesome when Qui was gone. They were frightened, too. There were no cousins around, and very few Vietnamese.

Less than 100 miles away, the war was raging in Vietnam's Mekong Delta and in the Central Highlands. The fighting also was spilling over into southern Cambodia.

By December 1971, Cambodia was aflame. The capital was shelled by communist forces, the Khmer Rouge guerrillas had taken over the jungles, and U.S. bombers were dropping tons and tons of explosives and defoliants along the frontier.

Kampot suddenly was caught in the crossfire. The South Vietnamese (ARVN) and Cambodian troops poured mortars and rockets onto the once-charming village. The Viet Cong, North Vietnamese and Khmer Rouge struck back. Squadrons of U.S. B-52s from Thailand bases thundered overhead, dropping their awesome payloads.

Qui hadn't been home since the communists shelled the port of Kompong Som. Sang was 10 and Cuc was just six years old when they left their home on the hill and became refugees of the expanding war.

Hoa and her children set out in search of Qui, whose ship was moored on the high seas, somewhere between Kep and Ha Tien, Vietnam. They followed the highway along the coast, through the acrid ruins of tiny villages which had been bombed into oblivion.

It was about midnight on the second night when the skies were shocked white by flares. The forest floor trembled as rounds of artillery thudded and exploded all around. A burst of bullets splintered the trees just overhead.

Hoa jumped into a ditch and spread her body over her two children. For more than an hour, they laid there, trying not to move a muscle.

On the fourth day, they arrived in Kep, contacted Luu and boarded a 21-foot fishing vessel which pushed through the heavy seas for most of the night. At daybreak they saw Qui's ship.

The Huynhs were safe at sea. And they weren't going anywhere until it was safe on land.

After six months on the Gulf of Thailand, the Elephant Waters returned to the docks at Kompong Som. The scars of war were everywhere. Kampot was a city in shambles. But Sihanoukville had been mostly spared, and for awhile, it was a pleasant reprieve.

The outside world didn't learn of what happened at Phnom Penh on April 17, 1975, until years later. Six weeks before the fall of Phnom Penh, there were more than two million refugees packed into the once-gracious French colonial city.

Then the Khmer Rouge began the bombardment. Thousands of rockets were fired into the central city. Lon Nol was desperate. He ordered his air force to strafe the perimeter of the city and thousands of civilians died.

The Khmer Rouge guerrillas surged into the city. The war was over. A half-million people had died. The Asian holocaust was about to begin.

The Khmer Rouge ordered the evacuation of Phnom Penh so they could "clean up" the city. Then the loudspeakers told that a squadron of U.S. B-52s was going to bomb the city. Three million people were ordered to immediately move out.

The exiles – the Khmer Rouge called them "People of the Emigration" – were forced into camps on the outskirts of Phnom Penh.

They didn't know their fate. They only knew that something called "Angka Loeu" had declared that they would be starting over at the year zero.

Before the Khmer Rouge's nearly four-year reign of terror was ended by the invasion of Vietnamese armed forces, more than two million people – one out of every four Cambodians – had died.

Hoa's big sister Cam was one of them. Her husband Hun worked for Lon Nol's government. But before the fall of Phnom Penh, Hun fled to Saigon with his mistress.

The teen-age guerrillas were rounding up everyone who was associated with the Cambodian government. They broke into Cam's house, tied her hands behind her back and told her they were taking her to see "Angka." Then they slipped a plastic bag over her head and tied it tightly to her neck.

Cam squirmed and flailed as she was dragged toward a deep trench where she was pushed over the edge, her body sprawling atop a pile of writhing corpses. At least 50 bodies, some with gunshot wounds, some with crushed skulls, some with severed heads and others suffocated in plastic bags were piled in the ditch.

Cam's 16-year-old son was marched to the scene, and as he looked in horror at his mother's body, one of the soldiers smashed in his head with a club and he fell into the trench.

Before sunrise on April 19, some 150 miles to the south, the Huynhs received a wakeup call from the Khmer Rouge. Scores of guerrillas, with red and white bandanas tied around their necks and with most cradling automatic weapons were aboard a convoy of military trucks.

About 2,000 people were to be herded through the wilderness of forests and hills and lowland jungles by dozens of teenage boys in black pajamas, toting automatic weapons.

At noon on the fifth day, the Huynhs were given their assignment. They along with nine other families were to tame about 100 acres of jungle. Qui and Sang built a hut out of bamboo sticks before the monsoon rains turned the jungle into quagmire.

The teenage guerrillas took interest in Sang. "Angka needs him," one soldier said as he prodded Sang along with his AK-47 toward the camp headquarters.

Months went by and there was no word about Sang. Hoa was sick with worry. Sang was mature for his age, but still he was only 13. Was he now a Khmer Rouge guerrilla?

Loudspeakers blared incessant propaganda messages. The mid-day feeding stations especially were used to intimidate, if they couldn't convert, the "new people" to the mindset of the Khmer Rouge.

Angka Loeu was the deity of the Khmer Rouge. It was the evil spirit that guided the Cambodian apocalypse. Hundreds of thousands were slaughtered in its name to create the utopian society in the new Kampuchea. It would be a Maoist-styled agricultural commune, a society where illiterate peasants were the ideal and educated city folks were the enemy.

The majority of the two million victims of the Cambodian holocaust died of illness and starvation when they were uprooted from their cities and villages and were forced to work in the harsh interior of the country. An estimated 200,000 were executed by the Khmer Rouge. They included most of Cambodia's educated elite, physicians, engineers, trained technicians, religious leaders and ethnic minorities.

The Angka Loeu diabolic scheme came to a halt on Christmas Day in 1978, when the Vietnamese army, after a series of border clashes, launched an offensive, crossed into Cambodia and in a lightning invasion captured Phnom Penh on Jan. 7, 1979. Pol Pot and his guerrillas fled to the jungles of the northwest, where they were supported by strange bedfellows: China and the U.S., both foes of Vietnam.

There were more than 600 youths in the Khmer Rouge camp. Many were younger than Sang. He was issued a black pajama uniform. He was told he'd get his red bandana later, if he passed muster.

Every morning the recruits learned guerrilla tactics, how to kill with a knife or choke with a cord or strangle with their bare hands. Every afternoon they were indoctrinated with the philosophy of Mao. Every evening they were led into the jungle to learn survival skills.

After two months of intensive combat training and grueling work in clearing the jungles for rice paddies, and hours upon hours of Mao and Pol Pot propaganda, the Khmer Rouge youth brigade was ready to move out. It was early September and the young guerrillas were to be assigned to military units throughout the country.

One evening Hoa had shivers as she watched two soldiers walk down the path to their hut. Did they have news of Sang? Were they now after Cuc to serve in the Khmer Rouge brigade?

"Is your family Vietnamese?" the soldier asked. "We're all Cambodian," Hoa said defiantly in Khmer. "Why do you ask?"

"We've been sent to look for Vietnamese ethnics," he said. "They're going to be exchanged for Khmer Rouge prisoners now held in Vietnam."

Hoa hesitated, then blurted out, "Yes, we're all Vietnamese. We've never lived there but we speak Vietnamese and follow the customs of our ancestors."

"Why didn't you say so," the soldier said angrily.

"Because I thought we'd be killed," Hoa said.

"A week ago you would have been killed," he said. "But now you Vietnamese are worth something. We'll send you three to Vietnam and we'll get back three Khmer Rouge soldiers."

For the first time in years, Hoa felt empowered instead of afraid. "There are four of us. Our son Sang was taken away three months ago to be trained as a Khmer Rouge soldier."

Hoa took a deep breath and said, "We aren't going anywhere without our son."

There were about 300 Vietnamese awaiting the prisoner exchange in Kampot. Most were anxious to leave Kampuchea at any cost. But

Hoa was able to convince 30 of them to sign a petition saying they wouldn't leave without her son Sang.

The Khmer Rouge official glared at Hoa across his desk. Then he said, "We've found your son. He's on his way. Here are your papers. You're all free to go to Vietnam."

Thousands of Khmer Rouge guerrillas had been captured by the Vietnamese militia after countless incursions into southern Vietnam. Pol Pot's forces were fierce but few. He needed those POWs to shepherd his diabolic plan into the interior to remake Kampuchea into a Maoist agricultural commune.

The next day, a truckload of Khmer Rouge soldiers pulled up to the headquarters. Sang jumped over the tailgate before the truck came to a stop, stripping off his bandana and pajama top as he ran.

The Huynhs were on their way to Vietnam, at last.

The long nightmare was over. The bus lumbered into Rach Gia, Vietnam, and was met by dozens of relatives and friends. It was Sept. 10, 1975, when the Huynh family first stepped on Vietnamese soil, just five months after the communist takeover.

It wasn't the Vietnam they had dreamed of. Hanoi had sent in its communist cadre to run the Mekong Delta and they made their presence known.

Qui joined his brothers in the fishing industry, and the business was good – until communist officials confiscated their three boats. Even though the northerners never credited the Viet Cong for their efforts in the war, they were granted the right to retaliate against their southern foes.

Two former Viet Cong soldiers stole Sang's motorcycle at gunpoint, in full view of the communist police officers. Then the police chief entered their house and took their television set, saying the Huynhs didn't deserve to have one.

Hoa was steaming. "We don't have a country," she said to her husband. "We're not Cambodian and were not Vietnamese either. I think we should get out of here."

North and South Vietnam formally became unified in July 1976. But the nation was far from being united. The country was devastated. Forests and fields had been poisoned by defoliants and Agent Orange. Nearly one million Viet Cong and North Vietnamese troops were dead. About 200,000 ARVN troops were killed in combat. A half million civilians died and a million more were maimed. The American death toll officially totaled 58,183 and 300,000 were injured.

On the eve of the fall of Saigon in April 1975, thousands of South Vietnamese, ranking military officers, their families and those who worked for the Americans were evacuated by helicopters to a U.S. fleet of ships awaiting in the South China Sea. In the initial wave, more than 130,000 Vietnamese fled their country.

At first the communist soldiers and police tried to halt the exodus. Then as the government tried to purge dissidents and malcontents – and wealthy businessmen with properties ripe for confiscation – the authorities not only winked at the escapees but they controlled a piece of the action.

There was money to be made in the refugee trade.

The price of passage was $3,000 in gold and thousands of wealthy ethnic Chinese stood in line to leave Vietnam. It was a billion dollar business and Rach Gia, the home of "Rust Bucket Tours, Inc.," was conveniently located on the Gulf of Thailand, in reach of Malaysia, Indonesia and Thailand.

More than 50 new boats were built in Rach Gia specifically for the refugee trade. One of the refugee entrepreneurs was a familiar Chinese businessman. Chan Luu, the owner of the "Elephant Waters," had moved his operations to Vietnam. He was in the process of building a fleet of wooden ships that would carry at least 100 passengers each.

Sang and Qui would become key to Luu's operation. Qui oversaw the building of boats at Long Xuyen and Sang recruited and delivered passengers from Saigon to Rach Gia. He received $100 for each refugee and in the first year he delivered 1,000 passengers.

But Sang soon became a marked young man. The police patrol threatened him with a long prison term if he was ever caught in the presence of refugees.

On April 6, 1981, just two days after Sang was confronted by police in the Rach Gia harbor, an official delivered a dreaded letter to his house. It read: "You have been inducted in the Vietnamese Revolutionary Army. You are to report next Monday to the processing center in Rach Gia."

The Huynh extended family of seven left Rach Gia that night. They included Qui and Hoa, their son Sang and daughter Cuc, Sang's teenage wife Dung and their infant son Sang and Dung's ailing brother Giang.

They boarded a 21-foot shuttle scow to reach Luu's largest vessel, moored 10 miles out in the Gulf of Thailand. There was no moon, and fog was rising from the gulf as the police patrol opened fire toward the sound of their boat's engine. A spray of bullets slammed into the wooden scow, just missing Hoa who was cradling her infant grandson.

Sang cut the engine, and the boat bobbed and drifted out to sea to his familiar rendezvous site. The Huynhs had been told they would board a big, fast boat that would reach the shores of Thailand within two days. Instead, the only available vessel was a 27-foot wooden boat, overcrowded with 37 passengers.

They spent 10 long days on the sea, through storms and blazing sun, and survived an attack by pirates armed with AK-47s who assaulted the women and stole their gold and jewels.

At last they were safe on the shores of Thailand, and were headed to a United Nations' refugee camp. Like thousands of others, they were hoping to land a sponsor and a ticket to America.

By spring 1981, six years after the fall of Saigon, nearly one million Vietnamese had become refugees. Before the second and third waves were over, the United Nations estimated that 1.8 million people had fled Vietnam.

Thailand was growing weary of putting up so many refugees, several camps had been shuttered and refugees had been returned to Vietnam. Sponsor lists also were thinning, and large family groups were having difficult times finding sponsors. The Huynh extended family of seven was shuttled around in several camps for almost five months. Officials suggested they split up, and be agreeable to be resettled in Australia or France to have a better chance of finding a sponsor.

Hoa ended the conversation. She declared the family members would stay together. And they would go to America.

By the end of the month, the Huynh family of seven was on its way to Neenah, Wisconsin, thanks to an ecumenical sponsorship. Members of the First Presbyterian Church, who had applied for a family of four, contacted the Catholic parish across town, St. Margaret Mary's, to jointly sponsor the seven.

The Catholics and the Presbyterians gathered at the Appleton airport to greet *Chao Mung* to the Huynhs, animists and Buddhists. It was a chilly autumn evening in 1981 when they arrived in downtown Neenah, and snow was on its way.

That winter was one of the most severe in state history. Neenah registered more than 100 inches of snow and 50 below-zero days. Most of the Huynhs dreamed of going to California where a majority of the Vietnamese refugees had settled.

But Hoa wouldn't hear of it. She said the family owed a debt of gratitude to their sponsors. Neenah was to be their home.

But after the family's 35 years in America, only Hoa remained in Neenah. She couldn't leave her sponsors or her husband Qui, who was buried at Oak Hill Cemetery.

Resource:

Peter A. Geniesse, "Cuc: Flower of the Delta," A Viet Kieu Odyssey, iUniverse, Inc., 2004.

CHAPTER TWENTY-FIVE

Photos by Peter A. Geniesse

Alejandra Anacleto Gregorio celebrated her *quinceañero* **in the village of Citlaltepec, Veracruz, Mexico, after undergoing a medical miracle in Wisconsin which saved her life and her smile.**

"We all know that it was divine intervention, aided by the skilled hands of the medical team. We feel truly blessed to be witness to this miracle."
—Leticia Santiago

CHAPTER TWENTY-FIVE

ALEJANDRA'S MIRACLE

Citlaltépec, Ver., Mexico   2011

They knelt on the cold, tile floor, unflinching for hours. Tears welled up in their eyes as they tried to focus upon the statue of the Blessed Virgin. A field of candles flickered throughout the cavernous crypt that held crutches and canes and messages of gratitude from pilgrims of long ago.

Leticia and Alejandra had come to The Chapel at Robinsonville to pray for a miracle.

They knew very little about the modest shrine near Champion, 17 miles northeast of Green Bay, Wis., where the Blessed Virgin appeared to a young, handicapped Belgian girl named Adele Brise back in 1858.

All they knew was that the shrine had recently been declared "worthy of belief" by the Catholic Church.

It's the first shrine in the U.S. to make the grade, putting The Chapel in the company of Lourdes, Fatima and their favorite, Our Lady of Guadalupe, among a half-dozen other sites in the world.

Both Leticia and Alejandra grew up in indigenous Mexico, faithful to the Virgin Mary's promises and believers of her apparitions to an Indian peasant named Juan Diego back in 1531.

Earlier that year, the two had prayed on their knees for a miracle at the altar of the world-renowned basilica outside of Mexico City that draws 10 million pilgrims every year. But it was not to be.

On that Saturday afternoon in late February 2012 they were light years away from that source of their faith, and they needed God's graces more than ever. So together they prayed at the Shrine of Our Lady of Good Help, a spiritual oasis in a rural cornfield.

A day later, their prayers were answered.

She wasn't cured of her affliction outright. She still faced more than three months of scary blood spurts and emergency treatments. Just when she felt that she was making real progress, she'd be rushed to the hospital once more.

The miracle they prayed for was named hope. The team of surgeons at Milwaukee's Children's Hospital which once turned her away had given Alejandra another chance.

Alejandra had third-stage-plus Arteriovenous Malformation, commonly known as AVM. Doctors gave her a year to live, at best. And that's why they delayed and deferred treatment. The outcome just wouldn't warrant the effort – or the cost. Besides, there was a strong chance that she wouldn't survive surgery.

They didn't feel obligated to treat the teenager. She wasn't their patient. After all, if she hadn't already arrived in the United States, they wouldn't have even considered her case.

But on that Sunday afternoon in late February, a medical emergency was declared. And when that happens, there's no time to debate, to assess solutions, or to weigh costs.

Alejandra's facial lesion was hemorrhaging and the bleeding wouldn't stop. Leticia, her foster mother and legal guardian, rushed her to the emergency room at Theda Clark Medical Center in Neenah, Wis., like she had done many times before.

The nurses applied pressure and wads of gauze but the blood continued to ooze and spurt. Alejandra desperately pressed her fingers about the wound and her eyes were filled with fear.

The emergency room physician that day, Dr. Andrew Schmitt, said his team wasn't equipped to deal with AVM. There were only a handful of physicians in the U.S. who could, he said. One team was at Children's Hospital in Milwaukee. Alejandra would have to be airlifted there. She couldn't survive ground transportation.

The ThedaStar helicopter was standing nearby, but Schmitt opted for the helicopter from Children's Hospital and secured the patient approval from Dr. Beth Drolet, director of the Vascular Anomalies Center. It took 15 minutes for the ambulance crew to land in Neenah. They had a tailwind. A half-hour later, she was in the care of Milwaukee's AVM specialists.

They had seen Alejandra before, but they didn't deem hers an emergency case. This time, it was different.

Dr. Craig Johnson, an interventional radiologist, spoke softly to Alejandra in Spanish. Then as he was preparing Alejandra to have an angiogram, an artery burst. He waved off the nurses and applied pressure on the wound for 45 minutes until his fingers went numb. At last the bleeding stopped.

The next day Johnson embolized, or blocked, the six main arteries that were fed by both carotid arteries. The intricate procedure took seven hours. He feared he would lose her. It also was likely she would be blind in one eye, or maybe it would leave her mouth permanently ajar.

The medical team anxiously awaited Dr. Johnson's return from the surgical theater. The results were encouraging, he said. Alejandra then was put into an induced coma.

Leticia was at Alejandra's bedside when she emerged from the coma the next day. She recalled how faith-filled the girl was before she went into surgery. Alejandra had so many close calls that she was no longer afraid. She often talked of heaven and of meeting Jesus.

Long before she arrived in Milwaukee, she had dreamed of being cured in the U.S. She had a vision of her brother Francisco asking Pope John Paul II to come to the aid of his sister. In the dream, the pope looked at Alejandra and said, "I will help you, but you will have to go to the United States."

Leticia was curious about what Alejandra might have remembered during the life-saving procedure that took nine hours. Alejandra slowly reconstructed bits of a dream. She said she had seen Jesus two times.

In her dream, all her brothers and sisters were gathered at their home in Citlaltépec, Mexico, when she was blinded by a white light as Jesus walked into the room. On another occasion Alejandra related that while she and her mother were walking in the yard, a man appeared who called her by name. She didn't recognize him until her mother said, "That's Jesus, the Almighty."

Alejandra could relate to Adele Brise's story. The young woman was blind in one eye and her face was disfigured from an accident with liquid lye when she was a child growing up in Belgium. She was handicapped, frail and reclusive, and wanted to stay home and become a nun.

She was 24 when she came to America in 1855 with her parents, settling in northeastern Wisconsin with the first wave of 15,000 Belgian immigrants.

Adele was a loner. She couldn't read or write. But she was pious and had a strong faith. Every Sunday morning she would walk several miles along an Indian trail to attend Mass at Bay Settlement.

On the morning of April 15, 1858, as she was passing through the woods at Robinsonville, she was overpowered by a blinding white light, which evolved into a beautiful woman in dazzling white garments. She bore a radiant and kindly smile. Adele trembled with fear as the vision faded away.

The following Sunday she walked the same path along with two companions. When they reached the site, Adele collapsed to her knees as the apparition reappeared. Her friends saw nothing unusual. For the next several weeks, curious crowds followed Adele through the woods each Sunday.

Then on Oct. 9, 1858, her friends saw Adele once again fall to her knees at the site and ask aloud, "In the name of God, who are you and what do you wish of me?"

"I am the queen of the heavens who prays for the conversion of sinners," she said in a soft voice. "I want you to do the same." The visionary woman told Adele, an illiterate peasant, to start a religious school for the region's children who lived miles away from any teacher.

She felt unqualified, and initially she was rejected by church authorities. But Adele succeeded in raising enough funds to start a school and build a tiny chapel on the site of the apparitions.

When she was rejected by authorities and scoffed at by skeptics, Adele turned to the Lord and miracle cures began to occur at the chapel. Tales of blind visitors regaining sight, of desperately sick being cured and of cripples restored to health began to spread.

Adele gathered a group of like-minded women and founded a Third Order community and opened a boarding school named St. Mary's Academy alongside the chapel.

Then on Oct. 8, 1871, firestorms engulfed the region in flames on both sides of the bay of Green Bay. In the historic conflagration, some 2,400 square miles were destroyed and an estimated 2,000 people died. It started in Peshtigo – the same day as the Chicago fire – and spread easterly across the bay for 40 miles to reach Robinsonville.

As the flames whipped by strong winds grew near, Adele and her companions gathered at the site and carried a statue of the Blessed Virgin in an endless procession around the grounds. They were joined by hundreds of pilgrims fleeing the fires. They prayed the rosary and they fell to their knees, and they were spared.

The next morning, when the fire ebbed and the fields and forests were turned to ashes, all the houses and barns in the neighborhood were destroyed. Except for the school, chapel and fences that encompassed the six acres consecrated to the Blessed Virgin. They were untouched, a green grass oasis in the midst of the smoldering landscape.

Sister Adele died in 1896 at the age of 65 and is buried at the entrance to the church crypt. Her legend lives on. For more than 150 years, thousands of pilgrims from all over have attended an outdoor Mass on Aug. 15, the feast of the Mary's Assumption into Heaven, and then processed, praying the rosary along the perimeter of the sacred grounds.

There were years when crowds numbered more than 25,000 and the celebrants included Catholic bishops and cardinals. In recent times the attendance had been more modest, but the Belgian community still claimed The Chapel as its own.

In 2009, the Diocese of Green Bay launched an official investigation to review the facts and circumstances of Adele's encounters with the Virgin Mary. On Dec. 8, 2010, Bishop David Ricken announced that the Marian apparitions were "worthy of belief."

Since that time, bus loads of pilgrims have traveled to Champion from all over the United States to pray at Adele's sacred site.

Alejandra was born with AVM. Most victims are treated as infants. But she was the youngest of 10 children, growing up in abject poverty in a remote mountain village. There were no hospitals nor clinics nor even nurses.

She had a facial disfigurement which often drew stares. The left side of her face resembled a pock-marked purple sponge, stretching from eye to mouth. Sometimes it would bleed and she would hide and cry.

Alejandra became ever more withdrawn when she went to school. She was smart, a good student, but extremely shy. She often covered her face with a notebook when she left class. When visitors came to her house, she would hide behind her mother.

That is how Leticia Santiago got to know Alejandra Anacleto Gregorio.

Leticia also is from Citlaltépec, a remote village in the Sierra Madre Oriental foothills, about 200 miles north of Veracruz and 300 miles south of Brownsville, Texas. She came to the United States in 1996, went to college, married and became a U.S. citizen. But she never forgot her hometown. She took a job teaching Spanish at St. John's School in Little Chute, Wis., and when the school was looking for a mission to support, she nominated her village.

Over the years, more than $70,000 was raised to assist schools, the Catholic parish and impoverished students in Citlaltépec. More than 100 families in the Little Chute area sponsored students, providing uniforms, backpacks and school supplies.

One of those students was Alejandra.

Leticia returned to her village each year to visit her family. At the same time she personally met and delivered donated items to the students and their families.

She couldn't help but notice Alejandra who hid her face and stood behind her mother each time they met. Some of the more needy students received additional help and Leticia often wished there was something she could do to help Alejandra.

In 2007, Leticia escorted a contingent from Little Chute to visit Citlaltepec, the village's Sister City. Among them was Sarah Wydeven, a senior at Little Chute High School, who drew widespread support for her "Backpacks without Borders" campaign. They were accompanied by her sister Nicole and her mother, Peggy Wydeven, When they met Alejandra, they became determined to bring her to the U.S. for constructive surgery.

It took four years to secure a U.S. visa and various sponsorships, including Healing the Children, a Milwaukee-based agency, along with arranging for physicians and medical facilities. All the services were pledged pro-bono.

Alejandra arrived in the U.S. with Leticia on Sept. 12, 2011. The family of five, including her husband Peter and three young boys, made room for Alejandra in their three-bedroom house in suburban Appleton, Wis.

A plastic surgeon from Neenah, Dr. Todd Van Ye, with only photos for reference, indicated he could complete the treatments and have her home before Christmas.

But it wasn't until Van Ye examined her that he discovered she had been misdiagnosed in Mexico. Instead of a birth defect called hemangioma, he said she had a high flow vascular malformation. AVM is an abnormal connection between arteries and veins, bypassing the capillary system.

Alejandra was judged a poor surgical candidate. The case was referred to Dr. Joseph Introcaso, an Appleton, Wis., intervention radiologist, who presented a treatment plan that included a series of embolizations followed by radiation therapy. However, he didn't have medical team support for the procecdures.

Alejandra was brought to Children's Hospital of Wisconsin to be evaluated by a team of eight physicians at the Vascular Anomalies Center. However, Healing the Children agency said it couldn't support the medical team's surgical treatment plan due to the high risk to Alejandra's life and the lack of follow-up treatment back in Mexico.

So, after nearly six months of tests, consultations and differing options, Alejandra still hadn't received a single treatment.

Her condition had worsened and the bleeding episodes became more frequent, sometimes almost a daily occurrence. Once an artery burst in the early morning hours while she was in her bed. Blood sprayed throughout the room, the carpet and walls and all over the bathroom. Once again she was rushed to the Theda Clark's emergency room.

In desperation, contacts were made with a radiologist in Colorado and with the Children's Hospital of Boston, both experienced in the treatment of AVM. Mayo Clinic in Rochester, Minnesota, also was approached. But no one stepped forth to take on Alejandra's case.

Alejandra's parents urged her to come back home. After all, six months had passed and their daughter was worse off. Alejandra insisted that she stay in the U.S. for treatment. Besides, the doctors said she was in no condition to travel. Leticia's family was worried that she might die in the U.S. without being cared for. She received the last rites from a priest in Appleton.

Leticia reminded Alejandra of their visit to the Basilica of Our Lady of Guadalupe before they left Mexico. She told her that God and the Blessed Virgin would be with her every step of the way.

But now they were in Wisconsin, thousands of miles away. And hope was fading fast.

Leticia's in-laws were vacationing in Door County in late February. They had taken the grandchildren for an over-night stay and now were returning them to their parents. Her mother-in-law suggested the families meet halfway on the way to Appleton. Perhaps, they could say a prayer at The Chapel at Robinsonville, which was sacred ground for her husband's Belgian relatives.

Leticia and Alejandra prayed on their knees in the crypt. And they held hands and cried together.

The following day their prayers were answered.

The team of physicians just couldn't let her die.

"There's no doubt in my mind that God intervened when all the doors seemed closed to getting help for Alejandra," Leticia said. "There's no doubt it was a medical miracle."

The treatments went on for hours at a time and stretched over the course of three months at Milwaukee's Children's Hospital. There were setbacks and bleeding episodes and there were times when the specialists feared Alejandra might lose vision in one eye and forever be on a feeding tube.

But they were undaunted by the challenge. Some came to realize they were inspired and achieving far beyond their capabilities.

Each day, the doctors and nurses rallied around Alejandra's bed. She became their favorite patient. Each day, there were miracles, big and small. She could smile and she liked what she saw in a mirror.

On March 24, four weeks after Alejandra had arrived at Children's Hospital in Milwaukee, Dr. Johnson and Dr. John Jensen, the plastic surgeon, struggled with a life-threatening decision. They would have to do major surgery to assure that Alejandra wouldn't have future bleeding episodes.

After eight hours in surgery, the nidus, or center of the lesion, the source of all bleeding, was successfully removed. Dr. Jensen said if they had attempted to perform that procedure back in December, Alejandra surely would have died on the table.

"The approach we took to treat her through embolization is what may have saved her life," Dr. Jensen said.

Leticia said, "We know that it was divine intervention, aided by the skilled hands of the medical team. We feel truly blessed to be witness to this miracle."

Alejandra was discharged from the hospital on March 30. She returned for checkups and touchups over the next six weeks.

On May 20, Alejandra and Leticia and her family once again visited the Shrine of Our Lady of Good Help at Champion, Wis., in thanksgiving for her cure.

Eight months after they were told that she would be cured by Christmas 2011, Leticia and Alejandra were back in Mexico. They made a pilgrimage to the Basilica de Nuestra Señora de Zapopán near Guadalajara where they had prayed a year earlier and then returned to Mexico City to meet with Alejandra's parents and to give thanks at the altar of Our Lady of Guadalupe.

That August, Leticia was back in her hometown of Citlaltépec to help celebrate Alejandra's 15th birthday, her *quinceañera*, the most important fiesta for a teenage girl. She walked down the aisle of San Nicolás Church in a robin-egg blue dress, escorted by a six teenage boy attendants, and greeted hundreds of guests, danced and posed for photos at the banquet hall.

No one could believe it was the same shy girl who hid from view for all her life. There was not a single mark on her face to remind them of her recluse past.

That fall, Alejandra was back in school, singing in the choir and playing soccer. She had become a village celebrity of sorts. She joined a prayer group and the parish priest recruited her to carry the cross in procession to the 14th station atop a hill on Good Friday.

Through much of her ordeal in the U.S., she would talk about wanting to become a doctor to pay back society for all that was done for her. Sometimes the conversation centered on God's call and whether the convent might be a better place for her.

One day in July 2015, a group of nuns gave a presentation at San Nicolás Church on following in the footsteps of Jesus. Alejandra had just turned 18, and had completed secondary school, graduating with honors. She was ready to map out her life.

It didn't take much convincing for her. She's now a member of the *"Amigas de Jesús,"* a contemplative order of nuns whose mission is to pray and serve the poor. In late 2015 she was welcomed into the novitiate by the bishop of Texcoco, a diocese near Mexico City.

CHAPTER TWENTY-SIX

Photo by Peter A. Geniesse

Humanitarian groups from throughout the U.S. each year trek the Migrant Trail through the Sonora Desert in memory of thousands of Latinos who have died trying to get to the U.S.

"I don't know what to do. I'm all alone. My family and community are counting on me to get a job in the U.S. and send back money."
–José Luis

CHAPTER TWENTY-SIX

'ILLEGAL ALIEN' JOSÉ LUIS

1995-2009?
Altar, Sonora, Mexico   2009

He was a small Indian boy, all alone and two thousand miles from home. He was slumped on a bench in the shade of the town square. He said he was 14 and was from Oaxaca, Mexico, and he was heading to California to pick grapes.

His family lived in Cienguilla, a remote mountain village, and spoke Chatino. He was the only member to speak Spanish, the only one to go to school. So he was selected to go to the United States. Oaxaca's famed coffee crop had been decimated by the World Bank's actions. Someone had to feed his family.

He had never traveled farther than 10 miles from his mountain village. However, he had spent the previous two weeks on 3rd class buses, atop freight trains and trekking through the Sonoran desert. He was homesick and nervous, scared too, but he knew he'd have to carry on. Today he would cross the border into the United States, he said.

Back in Oaxaca, his family paid a *coyote* connection $300 to get José Luis through the U.S. border. He would then be on his own to get to Napa Valley where his cousin worked in the vineyards. He had but a few pesos tucked into his shoe. He had been robbed atop the "*Bestia*," the notorious freight train that had taken so many limbs and lives. He was still hurting after being attacked by a gang outside of Culiacán.

There were hundreds of boys like him in Altar that day. Many came from Chiapas, the indigenous southern-most state. Scores hung out together in the shade of *Nuestra Senora de Guadalupe* Church. The temperature hovered around 110 degrees Fahrenheit, and the wind whipped the grit like a blast furnace.

It was noon, and no one traverses the Sonoran Desert until the sun sets and the wind dies down.

A dozen windowless white vans were lined up off the town square, a tented cluster of shops selling water bottles, backpacks, shoes and dehydrated snacks, along with black clothing for night travel.

Altar is situated at the crossroads in the Sonoran Desert of major roads leading to Nogales and Tucson and to Mexicali and San Diego. Two decades ago it was a hot, dusty town that trucks rumbled through on their way to somewhere else. There were only two hotels and together they didn't make one star.

That was before fences went up on the U.S. frontier, and before millions of migrants began to surge along the border, searching for a gap in security to cross into the U.S.

By the year 2005, Altar saw as many as 3,000 migrants a day. The town's population had tripled, and almost everyone was involved in the migrant trade.

There were 15 hotels and 80 *casas de huespedes*, mostly overcrowded flop houses, to accommodate the migrants. Most of the guest houses packed dozens of men and boys on triple-stacked cubbyholes in a single room, charging each $5 a night. Taco stands and cheap eateries lined the dusty streets.

It was a seedy town, filled with *coyotes*, smugglers, drug dealers, and shady merchants, all targeting desperate young Mexicans and other Latinos.

José Luis felt vulnerable. There was no one he could trust. He hadn't slept in days, hadn't eaten much either. He was running out of money. He thought of going back to Ciengiuilla, but he couldn't afford a bus ticket. He started to cry when he was tapped on his shoulder by a priest in a long black cassock.

"*Hijo*," he said. "It looks like you could use a friend."

"*Sí, padre*, I don't know what to do. I'm all alone. My family and community are counting on me to get a job in the U.S. and send back money," he said. "I don't even know where I'm supposed to go or how to get there."

"I think you could use a good meal, a shower and a night's sleep in a clean bed," the priest said. "And I know just the place where you can get all that for nothing.

"By the way, where did you get that cap?" the priest asked. "That's the insignia of my favorite *futbol* team."

"It's mine, too, *padre*," José Luis said. "My uncle gave it to me for my birthday. He said it would bring me luck on my journey to the United States."

"Well, I pray it does," the priest said. "It's a dangerous journey. The people at the *Casa de Migrante* can tell you of the risks of crossing the desert by yourself. You should think about it. Maybe you shouldn't go this time."

"*Gracias, padre*, but I have to go."

"*Vaya con Diós*," the priest said as he leaned over and blessed José Luis' *futbol* cap.

The sun was setting and the wind had calmed as the drivers of the white vans revved their engines. The *coyotes* were rounding up their *pollitos*, stuffing 30 or more migrants into the back of each van.

"*Vámanos*, José Luis," his *coyote* hollered. "And stop listening to that priest. He doesn't know what he's talking about."

"*Adiós, padre*," José Luis called out, tipping his grey cap. "*Por favor*, say a prayer for me."

The caravan of vans processed down the sandy road, raising plumes of dust well into the distance. They were heading for Sásabe, Sonora, 50 miles away on the frontier. That border town, long a magnet for migrants, now had a formidable barrier halting passage to its twin town of Sásabe, Arizona.

The fence forces migrants to skirt the town onto more perilous terrain where the smugglers play an unending chess game with the U.S. Border Patrol. They stand on the sandy hills with binoculars and radios, monitoring the moves of agents more than a mile away.

One smuggler claimed he once successfully moved 14 groups of migrants into the U.S. in a single day. His cut was $100 a person.

Crossing into the U.S. is nearly impossible without a guide. A diligent *coyote* knows the location of the border cameras and the schedules of the Border Patrol. He knows the changing locations of the checkpoints as well as the off-road trails, gullies and animal trails to be followed.

José Luis didn't have the money to hire a guide. He scurried across the border when the *coyote* commanded, and trudged through the trail after a stream of migrants.

Some make the 75-mile journey from Sásabe to Tucson in three days. Most don't. They trek in cactus-filled gullies and travel mostly at night to avoid detection.

Some just don't make it.

Over the past half-century, I've traveled all over Mexico a couple of dozen times. Most trips were as a tourist. But in recent years, my visits were to gain a better understanding of the Mexican migrant.

I scouted the borderlands, from Matamoros to Nogales. I watched the walls go up and migrants climb over and around them. I witnessed the drug cartels' zones of terror, border patrol arrests and the *coyotes* with their *pollitos*.

I joined two Witness for Peace delegations to learn first-hand of the roots of migration, the push and pull of the U.S. I did discover an American shadow hovering over much of Mexico's misfortunes.

I stayed a couple of days with a Chatino-speaking family in Cienguilla, the same Oaxacan mountain village where José Luis was from.

I also spent a couple of nights at the *Casa de Migrantes* in Altar, the hostel sponsored by the Catholic diocese of Hermosillo. And I processed the Migrant Trail into the U.S., joining scores of humanitarians to get a feel for the journey and to be in solidarity with those who feel forced to leave their country.

For a dozen years now, as many as a thousand migrant activists of all ages have experienced the 75-mile trail through the Sonoran Desert from Sásabe to Tucson on the last weekend in May.

"We bear witness to the tragedy of death and the inhumanity in our midst," the Migrant Walk leaders say. "We make this sacred journey as a community, in defiance of the borders that attempt to divide us, committed to working together for the human dignity of all peoples."

It's a strenuous trip, grueling, dusty and there's nowhere to hide beneath the broiling sun. But our route was mapped out alongside a network of roads and highways. We had water trucks, food stations, medical people and emergency vehicles.

The migrants don't.

They follow tracks in the sand, skirting *arroyos*, and they climb rusty, barbed wire fences on remote cattle ranches. Most carry gallon jugs of water. They travel at night and rest during the day wherever they can find shade, always wary of their surroundings, snakes and vigilantes and the Border Patrol.

There are warnings posted of the dangers of the desert, and the human perils of the journey. The Mexican government distributes brochures which shout out in red ink that no one is free of the risk of dying. They warn that the coyotes lie about the conditions and the distance, saying that a jug of water ought to last the two-day trek.

There are handouts that urge migrants to anonymously report the location of corpses they might discover so that they can be recovered, identified and given a proper burial.

After two decades of death in the desert, the toll now stands at 6,000.

And yet they come. The number of migrants detained in the desert and deported to Mexico is staggering. Border apprehensions topped 1.6 million in the year 2000. The odds still favor the migrant reaching Tucson. For every 300 migrants apprehended, 1,000 make it through the desert gauntlet.

Before I left Tucson, I wanted to witness the U.S. side of the border. There were several humanitarian groups which fostered the migrants in southern Arizona. "Humane Borders" maintained 70 emergency water stations with towering blue flags on U.S. federal lands near the frontier with Mexico. "No More Deaths" and "Borderlinks" also were dedicated to the welfare of the migrants.

There also were anti-immigrant groups, most notably one vigilante unit called Minuteman American Defense which patrolled the desert, harassing and detaining migrants and referring them to the Border Patrol.

Then there are the ranchers who lease thousands of acres of sand, sagebrush and mesquite from the government to raise cattle. One typical spread of 64 square miles supports just 300 cattle. It lies right in the path of the migrants' trails.

I toured that ranch in a Jeep with the owner. The land, which stretched to the border, had been in the family for four generations. The rancher realized that migrants had little choice in following a route through the desert. Yet, he was upset to see his land trashed, his cattle troughs contaminated, his barbed wire fences cut and his herds scattered.

All along the *arroyos* there was evidence of the thousands of migrants who had crossed his land. It was where they discarded their plastic water bottles, their food packaging, their torn backpacks and their heavy clothing.

The rancher pointed out a nest of branches where he said he discovered a dead body. The desert, he said, is unforgiving. Some migrants get disoriented, he said, and die of thirst, or of heat stroke, or of hypothermia from the desert's night chills.

As I walked down the well-worn trail, I noticed a cap snagged by a thorn bush. It had the insignia from a Mexican soccer team. It looked a lot like the one José Luis wore.

Ten years earlier, I stood at a chain link border fence near El Paso, Texas, and locked a finger with a Mexican teenager on the Ciudad Juárez side as we prayed together for an end to divisions and deaths in the desert.

We held white crosses with the names of migrants who had died trying to get to the United States. At that time the death toll was 2,800.

It was Nov. 2, 2003, "*El Dia de los Muertos*," and five bishops, from El Paso, San Antonio and Laredo, Texas and Las Cruces, New Mexico, concelebrated Mass with the bishop from Juárez, Chihuahua, who presided from across the border.

The Eucharistic altars, a pair of simple wooden tables, were separated only by a 12-foot chain link fence. A crowd, estimated at 500, equally divided on both sides, raised cardboard crosses with names of victims -- some labeled "unidentified" -- as they prayed for the end of that barrier.

It marked the fifth year that the bishops had concelebrated Mass on the border at nearby Anapra, N.M. It coincided with the week-long Border Pilgrimage, sponsored by two dozen religious and lay peace and justice organizations, including the Maryknoll Border Team, the American Friends Service Committee and Church World Service.

One leg of the Border Pilgrimage set out from Brownsville, Texas, and the other from San Diego. After five days of observations and interviews on both sides of the border, the groups merged in El Paso for reports and seminars.

They discovered that the U.S. border had never been so closed. At the same time economic conditions, fueled by NAFTA, the North American Free Trade Alliance enacted in 1994, had never made poor Mexicans so desperate to find jobs in the north.

That conflict pushed migrants into the deserts of the Southwest to cross over into the United States. Then came Sept. 11, 2001, immigration policy talks stalled and the terrorists' attacks led the U.S. to further tighten its borders in the name of national security.

A teenage Mexican boy gave testimony to the perils of crossing the desert to the pilgrims gathered in El Paso. He said he got lost and wandered deliriously for days without food or water before being rescued by a rancher. He started to cry as he told of becoming separated from his best buddy in the Chihuahua desert.

One of the pilgrims later related to the boy how he had found the remains of his friend.

The Border Pilgrimage forever changed my life. For the next decade I became an immigration activist which led to researching and writing "Illegal: NAFTA refugees forced to flee," that documents why millions of undocumented Mexicans have come to the U.S.

Epilogue

Over the course of a half century, I've written and published more than a million words. Much of it was the result of 40 years in the newspaper business as reporter and editor for two weeklies and two dailies. I wrote obituaries and editorials, I covered crime and city councils, and on occasion I wrote features, columns and investigative reports.

Ne'er did I receive a single nomination for a Pulitzer Prize.

Upon early retirement, I became a free-lance writer for a number of publications, newspapers and magazines, local and national. Then I penned a couple of books: **"Cuc: Flower of the Delta,"** a Viet Kieu odyssey of Vietnamese refugees, and **"Illegal,"** why millions of undocumented Mexicans have come to the U.S.

I did receive kudos for my support of refugees and immigrants. Indeed, their cause has become my passion. But nothing has given me more satisfaction in retrospect than this collection of stories of **Saints & Sinners.**

My occupation as journalist paid the bills, but my avocation as Third World scribe fed my soul. For a couple of weeks each year, often vacation time, I turned into a faux foreign correspondent. I used my press card to mingle with the mighty and the lowly to tell the folks back home what was happening in the land of the poor.

Oh, I liked to travel. At last count my passports sported stamps of more than 30 different countries. But it was the Third World that held a special allure. I was conflicted over why those countries were so impoverished and so often violent. There were so many untold stories.

The versions that played in the U.S. press all too often were filtered by the gringo psyche.

It all started back in the early 1960s in Cuernavaca, Mexico, when I met a modern-day prophet by the name of Ivan Illich. He nudged me away from rote answers and onto radical thinking. By the time I arrived in Antofagasta, Chile, as a lay missionary, I was primed to see the U.S. through Latin American eyes.

My first action was to side with Salvador Allende that Anaconda, a U.S. industrial behemoth, had no right to Chile's copper resources.

I also had no use for a general named Augusto Pinochet -- even in his early days in Antofagasta --who used the communism scare to score a military coup that resulted in the deaths of thousands of Chileans, including Allende.

Back in the U.S., I was troubled by President Reagan's Contra War in Nicaragua, especially since the state of Wisconsin had lined up on the other side. So I volunteered to go to Managua to try to make some sense of the dichotomy. I later traveled with Gail Phares' Witness for Peace group that essentially put an end to the ill-adventure.

I signed up for a journalist tour of Israel to try to figure out a Middle East peace plan and had coffee with Yitzhak Rabin. I was in Jerusalem for the Holocaust trial of "Ivan the Terrible" Demjamjuk who died before he could be convicted. Then, along came a story about Mordechai Vanunu, Israel's nuclear plant leaker.

My press card put me in a position to meet presidents and dictators including Nicaragua's Daniel Ortega, Cuba's Fidel Castro and Haiti's Jean-Bertrand Aristide.

I was in Chiapas, Mexico, when "Red" Bishop Samuel Ruiz rallied with the Zapatistas against NAFTA. Everywhere I traveled in the Third World I encountered the name Gustavo Gutiérrez, the liberation theologian, who set the stage for the Catholic Church's preferential option for the poor. I remember saying *"Presente"* at the School of the Americas when Archbishop Oscar Romero headed the litany of Latin American martyrs.

I was baptized in the Ganges in the cold waters of the high Himalayas by a famed Indian guru named Sant Keshavedas and I prayed with the Buddhists the day the Dalai Lama came to Madison, Wis.

It's a heady list of VIPs that I profiled for posterity. But there were others, not so widely known, who greatly impacted my adult life. Chile's 21ˢᵗ century saint, Alberto Hurtado, S.J., offered me his mantra: "It's very good not to do bad, but it's very bad not to do good."

Leo Mahon's experiment set the mission standard in Miguelito, Panama, and then there's Pat Pyeatt, my lay missionary colleague who studied for the priesthood and then switched to become a Sikh. Father "Beans" Bohnen, the saint of the Soleil slums, was truly inspirational as were the two young Haitian men I befriended who struggled against all odds to school their hometowns. Ferdinand Mahfood fed millions through his Food for the Poor in Haiti and Guyana and throughout the Caribbean.

I invested time and emotions in the lives of three others: a Vietnamese refugee woman who survived the killing fields of Cambodia; a 14-year-old migrant from Oaxaca, Mexico, who crossed the Sonoran Desert, and most likely didn't make it to California, and a Mexican teenage girl whose life was spared by medical miracles in the U.S.

Of all the people who helped change my world, one name forever stands tall: Father Ted Hesburgh, C.S.C. He wasn't of the Third World, but he was at home in it. The president of the University of Notre Dame for 35 years had a second career of 25 years as counselor to popes and presidents.

He was my hero – until Pope Francis came along.

I was a big fan of Pope John XXIII and of the Second Vatican Council which elevated the layman to sacred status. That was 50 years ago. It was a long drought for progressive Catholics.

"Panchito" was quickly penciled in as my favorite Latino and I was anxious to follow his footsteps. He was to be the final chapter, the climax of my career. I scored rare press credentials to cover Pope Francis' visits to Washington, D.C., New York and Philadelphia. But I never made it there.

I thought I might see him in Cuba. It was just a short flight from Toronto and I knew my way around Habana. It didn't happen.

Surely, we'd get together somewhere in Mexico. I'd been there a couple of dozen times and the Basilica of *Nuestra Señora de Guadalupe* was where I received my missionary cross in 1963.

I envisioned Pope Francis celebrating Mass on the frontier at Ciudad Juárez. In 2003 I took part in a pilgrimage along the border, praying for the thousands of migrants who had died in the desert trying to get to the U.S.

I never did see Pope Francis in person as he traveled the Americas in 2016. Age had something to do with it. At 78 I don't travel like I used to. But like millions of others, I watched his every move on television. And I sure liked what I saw.

About the Author

Peter A. Geniesse, 78, a native of Green Bay, Wis., and a graduate of the University of Notre Dame. worked as a reporter, editor and freelance writer for four newspapers and other publications over the course of five decades. He traveled extensively on assignments in Third World countries, especially throughout Latin America.